Daily
Words of
Comfort

Publications International, Ltd.

Contributing writer: Marie D. Jones
Cover art: Shutterstock.com
Interior art: Dreamstime, Getty, Shutterstock.com

Louis Weber, CEO
Publications International, Ltd.
8140 Lehigh Avenue
Morton Grove, IL 60053

ISBN: 978-1-68022-758-1

Manufactured in China.

8 7 6 5 4 3 2 1

Contents

Chapter 1

God Is Present

Yea, though I walk through the valley of the shadow of death, I will fear no evil: for thou art with me; thy rod and thy staff they comfort me.

—*Psalm 23:4*

$\mathcal{D}$ear God of comfort, I sense your loving presence all around me, in the ground beneath my feet, in the warming sun on my shoulders, in the gentle songs of the birds. You have made this world for us, your children, and the sight, sound, and touch of your creations comfort me as they surround me each day. Nothing can separate me from the joys of eternal life in you, just as nothing can separate me from the love you have shown for us in Jesus Christ.

And I heard a great voice out of heaven saying, Behold, the tabernacle of God is with men, and he will dwell with them, and they shall be his people, and God himself shall be with them, and be their God.
—Revelation 21:3

*L*ord, on days when everything seems to go wrong, help me to remember that you are always nearby to offer comfort. It is easy to get overwhelmed and feel lost and alone in this world, but deep down I know that is never the case. You are always at the ready to help—I just need to remember to take a moment to stop, breathe, and pray.

God's help is nearer than the door.
—Irish Proverb

*C*omfort me, O God, as I seek shelter from the storms of everyday life. I am grateful for the good I have, but sometimes feel I cannot carry the burden of life's challenges alone. Remind me with your loving presence that no matter what my day brings, you are there for me, with me, and on my behalf, making smooth the way before me. In your love I find rest.

Behold, God is my salvation; I will trust, and not be afraid: for the Lord Jehovah is my strength and my song; he also is become my salvation.

—Isaiah 12:2

*H*oly God, even in times of fear and uncertainty, please remind me that you surround me always. With every breath I take, let me breathe in your merciful love. With every blink of my eyes, let me see your comforting presence. With every beat of my heart, let me feel your spirit envelop me. I ask that you make me yours, totally and completely, and let me rest in the loving refuge of your arms.

Let us come before his presence with thanksgiving, and make a joyful noise unto him with psalms.

—Psalm 95:2

$\mathcal{L}$ord, how blessed we are to be able to see you all around us and to sense your presence within us. Even though we can't see you in the same way we might see a friend or a neighbor, we see you in your Word and in all that is good and true in the world around us. Thank you, Lord, for making yourself so available to us.

Let your conversation be without covetousness; and be content with such things as ye have: for he hath said, I will never leave thee, nor forsake thee.

—*Hebrews 13:5*

Anyone who has ever been abandoned deeply fears that they will be abandoned again. Often the worm of insecurity feeds the existing fear. It's a cycle of destruction that has no cure in human relationships. Even if our loved ones are faithful, still they are mortal. That's why God's promise to never leave or forsake us is such a powerful assurance.

God of comfort, how I need the security of your presence! You are truly the only one who can say that you will never abandon me. For you will be with me always: in life, in death, and in the life to come.

Where God is, our comfort and hope is. The divine presence blesses us when we walk in his light and do his will. We are bearers of light and love to all those we meet. We are his divinely inspired earthbound angels.

Abide with me,
fast falls the eventide;
The darkness deepens;
Lord, with me abide!
When other helpers fail
And comforts flee,
Help of the helpless,
O abide with me.
I need thy presence
Every passing hour;
What but thy grace
Can foil the tempter's power?
Who like thyself,
My guide and stay can be?
Through cloud and sunshine,
Lord, abide, with me.

—Henry F. Lyte

$\mathcal{D}$isaster can strike at any time without warning to anyone anywhere. Our lives can change dramatically in one unexpected moment, but in the worst times of our lives, we can lean on family, friends, and even strangers who reach out to us. Yet, even more importantly, we can turn to God, who is always there for us during our darkest hours. He will never fail us, never let us down, and never turn away from us when we cry out to him.

The wind bloweth where it listeth, and thou hearest the sound thereof, but canst not tell whence it cometh, and whither it goeth: so is every one that is born of the Spirit.

—*John 3:8*

$\mathcal{W}$hen the winds of change and challenge blow hard into my life, I will take refuge in you, O Lord. When the darkness descends upon my house and home, I will fear not for I will place my faith in you, O Lord. When my child is ill or my husband is hurt,

I will remain steadfast, for I know that you will be right there by my side, O Lord. Although I cannot see you, I know you are always with me, and in that I take comfort and find strength.

When my way is drear,
Precious Lord, linger near.
When the day is almost gone,
Hear my cry, hear my call,
Hold my hand, lest I fall,
Precious Lord, take my hand, lead me home.

$\mathcal{L}$ord, even when the storm is raging all around me, I feel your still, comforting presence. Thank you for letting me know that no matter how dark the skies and regardless of how high the water rises, you are always with me. You meet me in the midst of the storm, wherever you find me, and you calm my troubled spirit. And so, Lord, I praise you in this storm. For in it, I find you.

$\mathcal{O}$ God, the blessed feeling of being at home in your loving presence is like nothing else. The joy I feel when I know I never walk alone is the greatest of gifts, and when I look around at the wonderful people you have chosen to walk with me through life—my family and my

friends—I truly know that I am loved. No greater blessing exists than the feeling of being where we belong, with the people who make us happy, in the homes that bring us comfort and a sense of peace, doing work that makes us feel needed and satisfied. When we find our "true north," we feel at home and blessings await us behind each and every door.

Thou wilt shew me the path of life: in thy presence is fulness of joy; at thy right hand there are pleasures for evermore.

—Psalm 16:11

There is joy in being in God's presence. There is no other place we find joy in its fullness, shimmering in all its facets, except in the presence of God himself.

*Teaching them to observe all things whatsoever I have
commanded you: and, lo, I am with you always,
even unto the end of the world.*

—Matthew 28:20

The Bible promises that God will always be with us. Whether we are commuting to work, having coffee with friends, taking a walk, or even sleeping soundly through the night—whatever it is, wherever we are, he's there with us. He's the friend who always has time, never moves to another part of the world, is forever ready to listen, and provides the best counsel. It's just a matter of realizing he's there. The Gospel of Matthew closes with this powerful promise: "I am with you always, even unto the end of the world."

Almighty God, why is it we don't remember that you alone are the source of all comfort? Instead, when times are tough, we seek comfort in the things of the world that we see around us—in too much food, or drink, or late-night television. Those things can distract us, but we know they can never comfort us the way you do. Thank you for your faithfulness, God. For at the end of every one of our fruitless searches you are there, and in your presence we find true comfort.

Comforting God, blessed is your presence. For you and you alone give me power to walk through dark valleys into the light again. You and you alone give me hope when there seems no end to my suffering. You and you alone give me peace when the noise of my life over-

whelms me. I ask that you give this same power, hope, and peace to all who know discouragement, that they, too, may be emboldened and renewed by your everlasting love.

Jesus Christ the same yesterday,
and to day, and for ever.

—*Hebrews 13:8*

*L*ord Jesus Christ, what comfort we find in your changeless nature. When we look back and remember all the ways you've guided us in the past, we know we have no need to be anxious about the future. You were, are, and always will be our Savior and Lord. Why should we fear instability when you are always here with us?

Though long the weary way we tread,
And sorrow crown each lingering year,
No path we shun, no darkness dead,
Our hearts still whispering, thou art near!

—Oliver Wendell Holmes

O taste and see that the Lord is good:
blessed is the man that trusteth in him.

—*Psalm 34:8*

God, you are invisible but not unseen. You reveal yourself in creation and demonstrate your kindness in a stranger's sincere smile. You are intangible but not unfelt. You caress our faces with the wind and embrace us in a friend's arms. We look for you and feel your comforting presence.

O grace of my heart, I turn to you when I am feeling lost and alone. You restore me with strength, hope, and courage to face a new day. You bless me with joy and comfort me through trials and tribulations. You direct my thoughts, guide my actions, and temper my words. You give me the patience and kindness I need to be good. Grace of my heart, I turn to you. Amen.

But unto thee have I cried, O Lord; and in the morning shall my prayer prevent thee.

—*Psalm 88:13*

O Lord, this aloneness is almost more than I can take! If I could escape in a good night's sleep, I would. But my thoughts and fears and emotions are restless, hovering around this center of heartache. If it were not for you being here with me, I would despair. But your quiet presence keeps me from unraveling. These nights, these long drawnout nights of solitude, are where I find you waiting, ready to speak comfort to my heart and assure me that you have a future in store for me that is good and worth waiting for. Tonight, even if sleep eludes me again, I'll continue to rest in your love for me.

*S*ometimes when we feel like no one is on our side, we have to remind ourselves that no matter what obstacles of life crowd our path, we are never abandoned without an angel walking beside us.

The Lord is nigh unto all them that call upon him, to all that call upon him in truth.
—*Psalm 145:18*

*A*s we learn to trust you, God, we discover your strengthening presence in various places and people. Wherever we encounter shelter, comfort, rest, and peace, we are bound to hear your voice, welcoming us. And in whomever we find truth, love, gentleness, and humility, we are sure to hear your heartbeat, assuring us that you will always be near. Thank you, God. Amen.

We may be surrounded by friends and family, yet still feel so alone and misunderstood. Those around us may have their own problems and worries, leaving us feeling abandoned and unseen. But we are never truly alone, for God is always present. God's love is unceasing and unfailing, and we don't have to ask for it, or wait in line for it. We may forget God, but God never forgets us.

You never have to walk alone through life, because God walks with you. Whether your path is smooth and free of obstacles, or rough and filled with detours, God is there to help guide you and give you the strength to carry on and keep moving forward. There is no reason to feel lonely, and there is nothing to fear. God is there, now and always.

$\mathcal{I}$ can count on God to be there for me through thick and thin, good days and bad days, laughter and tears, joy and despair. No matter what I am experiencing, God is there to comfort me and help me, and even to point out the lessons I was meant to learn along the way. I can count on people to be there for me some of the time, but only God is reliable 24 hours a day, 7 days a week, 365 days a year.

$\mathcal{W}$hen all is said and done, God remains. Love interests will leave us, family and friends will move away or pass on, and our children will grow to have lives of their own. Even our pets will one day be gone. But there is no reason to feel alone, or lonely, because God remains to walk with us on life's journey. God's presence has no shelf life or expiration date.

God will never leave thee,
All thy wants He knows,
Feels the pains that grieve thee,
Sees thy cares and woes.
Raise thine eyes to heaven
When thy spirits quail,
When, by tempests driven,
Heart and courage fail.
When in grief we languish,
He will dry the tear,
Who His children's anguish
Soothes with succour near.
All our woe and sadness,
In this world below,
Balance not the gladness,
We in heaven shall know.

—General Hymn #286,
Book of Common Prayer

This is our darkest hour when we feel we cannot suffer any worse. Yet, something inside whispers to us, "For everything there is a season," and we notice the faint glimmer of hope at the end of this long, dark tunnel of despair. The more we focus on the voice, the louder it becomes. The more we seek the light, the brighter it becomes. This is God's love and compassion for us making itself known, and in his growing presence, we become stronger and our faith is renewed.

$\mathcal{B}$e assured of God's presence as you weather this storm. As the waves toss you about, and the ship of your life threatens to crash into rough rocks: He is always there. Never despair. For no wind or water, rock or sand has the power to defeat his plans for you. And, after all, he created all these things.

$\mathcal{F}$riends come and go, but God remains. Life is filled with relationships with friends, family, and loved ones. Some of those will last a season or two, some may last forever. But the one true friendship we will never lose is the one we have with God. The presence of God does not come and go like the tides of the ocean. The presence of God is forever.

When I was a child, I had my favorite blanket. I took that blanket everywhere, wrapping myself in its warmth and comfort. Now I am all grown up, and you, God, are the one I turn to for that warmth and comfort. Like that blanket, I know all I have to do is call you and you will wrap your love around me and make me feel safe and snug. I am your child still, and no matter how old I get, I will always need you watching over me and making sure I am happy and secure. For you, God, are my permanent security blanket, my safe harbor from the storm, my rock, and my home.

I feel an old familiar panic coming over me, Lord. Comfort me now. As I breathe deeply, fill me with the knowledge that you are present and you are in control. Thank you, Lord. Only your intervention can calm my troubled soul.

To live a life of faith is to live always in God's comforting presence, at peace in the home of his love.

God's angels are messengers, giving us comfort and assurance of God's presence in any shadowy valley through which we may walk.

Chapter 2

Peace Be With You

Peace I leave with you, my peace I give unto you: not as the world giveth, give I unto you. Let not your heart be troubled, neither let it be afraid.

—*John 14:27*

And the peace of God, which passeth all understanding, shall keep your hearts and minds through Christ Jesus.

—*Philippians 4:7*

Dear God, I long to feel the comforting peace you bring, the peace that passes all understanding. Fill my entire being with the light of your love, your grace, and your everlasting mercy. Be the soft place that I might fall upon to find the rest and renewal I seek.

God of comfort, please send your peace to calm us when we're overwhelmed. Your presence wipes away depression and despair. It renews our hope and lifts our hearts. Amen.

Where there is peace, God is.
—George Herbert

Before me peaceful,
Behind me peaceful,
Under me peaceful,
Over me peaceful,
All around me peaceful.

Yes, Father in heaven,
often have we found that the
world cannot give us peace,
O but make us feel that thou
art able to give us peace;
let us know the truth of thy
promise: that the whole
world may not be able to
take away thy peace.

—Søren Kierkegaard

Behold, I will bring it health and cure, and I will cure them, and will reveal unto them the abundance of peace and truth.

—*Jeremiah 33:6*

Mental illness can be so devastating and stigmatizing, Lord. Few understand the heartaches involved in diseases that carry no apparent physical scars. Comfort those friends, neighbors, and family members who deal daily with difficult situations of which we are often unaware. Touch them with your special love, and let them know that they can lean on you, Lord. Ease their burdens, quell their sadness, and calm their desperation. Bring peace, comfort, and healing to these households. Remind them of the promise of your everlasting love.

Deep peace of the running waves to you.
Deep peace of the flowing air to you.
Deep peace of the smiling stars to you.
Deep peace of the quiet earth to you.
Deep peace of the watching shepherds to you.
Deep peace of the Son of Peace to you.

—Gaelic Prayer

I will both lay me down in peace, and sleep:
for thou, Lord, only makest me dwell in safety.

—Psalm 4:8

May He support us all the day long, till the
shades lengthen, and the evening comes, and
the busy world is hushed, and the fever of
life is over, and our work is done! Then in His
mercy may He give us a safe lodging, and a
holy rest, and peace at the last.

—*John Henry Newman*

Peace comes to those who know it is an inward state of mind, not an outward state of being. When we've attained inner balance and harmony, nothing that occurs outside of us can disrupt that calm. Those who have true peace of mind know that they can meet both good fortune and misfortune with a positive attitude and achieve an equally positive outcome. Inner peace depends not on outer circumstance, but on how we choose to react to it within.

Five enemies of peace inhabit with us—
avarice, ambition, envy, anger, and pride;
if these were to be banished, we should
infallibly enjoy perpetual peace.

—Petrarch

Peace in daily work is the consciousness of health and ability to spare so that when one's tasks are done there is a margin all around. Peace in business is the consciousness of capital and plenty, so that one need not fear what the day may bring. Peace in the family is the consciousness that, under all the strains inevitably incident to the running of a home, there is an unfailing wealth of love and devotion and fidelity to fall back upon. Peace in the soul is the consciousness that, however difficult life may be, we are not living it alone...

—Harry Emerson Fosdick

The words of wise men are heard in quiet more than the cry of him that ruleth among fools.

—Ecclesiastes 9:17

The world is a noisy place. From family to office to leisure and routes in between, the air vibrates with ear-grabbing, relentless chatter. I yearn for quiet conversations with the God of still, small voices. My spirit, like my body, is easily bruised by too much noise. Help me hear you, God of comfort. Help me shut out the world when you talk.

You calmed the stormy waters, God, and quieted the thunderous skies. I ask you to calm the stormy waters for me as I struggle with the challenges I face. I know that with the peace you provide, I can face any obstacle and get through any trial or tribulation before me. In the stillness within, you wait for me, always present, always ready to bring me safely back home as a lighthouse guides a ship through the cold, dark fog to the comfort of the shore. Thank you for calming my storms, God.

Depart from evil, and do good;
seek peace, and pursue it.

—*Psalm 34:14*

*B*less me with a peacemaker's kind heart and a builder's sturdy hand, Lord, for these are mean-spirited, litigious times when we tear down with words and weapons first and ask questions later. Help me take every opportunity to compliment, praise, and applaud as I rebuild peace.

Lord, make me an instrument of your peace, where there is hatred, let me sow love; where there is injury, pardon; where there is doubt, faith...

—St. Francis of Assisi

Let the peace of God rule in your hearts, to the which also ye are called in one body; and be ye thankful.

—*Colossians 3:15*

Sometimes we believe our souls can only be at peace if there is no outer turmoil. The wonder of God's peace is that even when the world around us is in confusion and our emotions are in a whirl, underneath it all we can know his peace.

49

*H*eavenly Father, our diversions seem great. We can't remember when the insurmountable demands started piling up, and we have a hard time seeing the end. Allow us to take a moment from our hectic days to close our eyes and feel your comforting peace. We ask you to lead us.

For to be carnally minded is death; but to be spiritually minded is life and peace.

—Romans 8:6

Lord, you are teaching me that finding peace requires me to seek it out—to look for and pursue peaceful places, peaceful ways, and peaceful relationships. If I make living in peace a priority, I won't miss it, and even when storms come my way I will know where to find rest and calm and quietude of spirit. Your Word so often pairs righteousness and peace. To live uprightly is to live in peace. Help me choose what is right and true and good today, as I seek to live in your peace, Lord.

Before prayer
I weave a silence on my lips,
I weave a silence into my mind,
I weave a silence within my heart.
I close my ears to distractions,
I close my eyes to attentions,
I close my heart to temptations.
Calm me O Lord as you stilled the storm,
Still me O Lord, keep me from harm.
Let all the tumult within me cease,
Enfold me Lord in your peace.

—Celtic Traditional

*L*ord, we often think of peace as something that comes when we're ready, when our hands are folded and our minds quiet. But your love and presence are in all things in this world, the loud and the quiet, the raging river as well as the silent pond. You are everywhere, and it is as easy to hear you on a bustling city street as it is in the isolated silence of a redwood forest. Please remind me that I can find your comforting peace anywhere, if my eyes are open and my heart is willing.

God, your peace is my cornerstone, upon which I build the foundation of my life. In your peace, I spread peace to my family and friends, and to my community, for this indeed is a world that needs more peace. Blessed am I to have found that peace in you, God.

First keep the peace within yourself,
then you can also bring peace to others.
                                    —Thomas à Kempis

*And he shall stand and feed in the strength of the
Lord, in the majesty of the name of the Lord his God;
and they shall abide: for now shall he be great unto
the ends of the earth. And this man shall be the peace,
when the Assyrian shall come into our land: and when
he shall tread in our palaces, then shall we raise against
him seven shepherds, and eight principal men.*

—Micah 5:4–5

There is a place of total calm and serenity we
can access at any time. That place is deep inside of
us, where God dwells in silence as an ever-present
reminder of his love. In this place, we experience
pure awareness of God's love, and our spirits are
renewed and refreshed. Even when life is loud and
distracting, we can come to this peaceful place
at any time.

God promises each of us the peace that passes all understanding. Imagine having a sense of calmness to carry with you throughout your day. Imagine always being able to tap into a wellspring of clarity and serenity whenever you need to. God's peace is beyond description, beyond understanding. God's peace is within us now.

Renounce all strength, but strength divine,
And peace shall be for ever thine.

—William Cowper

Sometimes life overwhelms me and I want to crawl up in a ball and hide away. But responsibilities and obligations do not allow me to, so I turn instead to God for help. He lightens my load and offers me peace, even amidst the stormiest days and nights. He takes my difficulties away, and replaces them with strength and resilience. When I turn to God, I am at peace and in the flow of his will for me.

The Lord lift up his countenance upon thee,
and give thee peace.

—*Numbers 6:26*

*H*ere is a place you can stop and rest for a while. Here is a place you can lay down your worries and let go of the weight of your fears upon your shoulders. Here is a place you can breathe deeply of fresh air, and feel the warmth of the sun on your skin. Here is a place filled with tranquility, like a beautiful garden. Here is where you are, with God.

God knows of your suffering and your troubles. God knows of your sorrow and your pain. God knows you seek peace from the turmoil of life and offers you his loving presence. It costs you nothing but the willingness to accept it. It is always available, day or night, just for the asking. When life grows difficult, God's peace washes over you like a gentle and comforting rain.

Surrender to the peacefulness of a day spent knowing you did your best. That is all God asks of you, that you offer your best and leave the rest to him. Knowing this, you can relax and not spend wasted time worrying about regrets of the past or concerns of the future, because each moment spent in alignment with God's will takes care of itself.

What is peace? Is it the absence of conflict, or the ability to stay calm and centered in God's love during the most trying of times? Peace is not something we only find at the end of a long battle. It is always available when we come to understand that with God on our side, there is never a battle to begin with.

The day was long, the burden I had borne
   Seemed heavier that I could no longer bear;
And then it lifted—but I did not know
   Someone had knelt in prayer.
Had taken me to God that very hour,
   And asked the easing of the load, and He
In infinite compassion, had stooped down
   And lifted the burden from me.
We cannot tell how often as we pray
   For some bewildered one, hurt and distressed,
The answer comes, but many times these hearts
   Find sudden peace and rest.
Someone had prayed, and faith, a lifted hand
   Reached up to God, and He reached down that day.
So many, many hearts have need of prayer—
   Then, let us, let us pray.

—Author Unknown

$\mathcal{L}$iving with stress causes so many health problems, not to mention strain on your mental and emotional state. Perhaps you cannot remove everything in life that causes you stress, but you can approach it with a sense of inner peace that makes you unshakeable and unstoppable. Life will never be perfectly calm, but as long as you are within, where God lives and moves and has his being, it won't matter what is happening on the outside.

God's peace is a bone-deep peace that calms every cell of the body. God's peace is a powerful peace that stops the storms within us and beyond us, and gently calls the spirit home to shore. God's peace is a comforting peace that soothes the heart-wounds whole again. God's peace is a bone-deep peace that quiets the restless soul.

Surely there is something in the unruffled calm of nature that overawes our little anxieties and doubts: the sight of the deep-blue sky, and the clustering stars above, seem to impart a quiet to the mind.

—Jonathan Edwards

Chapter 3

Words of Courage and Strength

God is our refuge and strength, a very present help in trouble.

—*Psalm 46:1*

*Be strong and of a good courage, fear not, nor be afraid
of them: for the Lord thy God, he it is that doth go with
thee; he will not fail thee, nor forsake thee.*

—*Deuteronomy 31:6*

We respond to stresses in our lives with either
fear or faith. Fear is a great threat to our faith.
That's why we read often in the scriptures the directive, "Fear not." The closer we draw to God, the
more our fears diminish.

Go forward with courage. When you are in doubt be still and wait; when doubt no longer exists for you, then go forward with courage. So long as mists envelope you, be still; be still until the sunlight pours through and dispels the mists— as it surely will. Then act with courage.

—Ponca Chief White Eagle

Lord, you do not leave us to suffer alone. You are with us in pain, in sickness, and in our worst moments. Thank you for your comfort and healing power. Thank you for getting us through when our bodies fail, when our health falters, and when we need you most of all.

*The Lord will give strength unto his people;
the Lord will bless his people with peace.*

—Psalm 29:11

*S*eeking courage, Lord, I bundle my fears and place them in your hands. Too heavy for me, too weighty even to ponder in this moment, such shadowy terrors shrink to size in my mind and—how wonderful!—wither to nothing in your grasp.

*L*ord, let me be strong today, drawing my courage from my hope in you. Help me lean not on my own strength but on your limitless power. I know there is work to be done—burdens to be lifted, temptations to be resisted, and unkindness to be forgiven. Let my thoughts and actions be motivated by the hope generated by your promises.

Whatever enlarges hope will also exalt courage.

—*Samuel Johnson*

I will love thee, O Lord, my strength. The Lord is my rock, and my fortress, and my deliverer; my God, my strength, in whom I will trust; my buckler, and the horn of my salvation, and my high tower.

—*Psalm 18:1–2*

Almighty God, what comfort I find in your constancy and faithfulness. You are the same God who hung the stars in the universe and called them by name. You've heard the prayers of troubled souls since the beginning of time, and yet you never stop listening. Thank you, Lord God, for your constant sovereignty and your unfailing love. You are indeed our comfort and our strength when everything else around us seems to be falling apart.

*F*ather in heaven, when all else fails, I turn to you for the comfort only you can provide. I have done all I can do, and now I rest in the belief that you are taking from me my burdens and doing for me what I cannot. In you alone do I find that comforting assurance that everything is being taken care of and that all will work out as it should. My surrender to your comfort is not out of weakness but out of my faith in your eternal love and concern for me. For that I am grateful.

Have courage for the great sorrows of life and patience for the small ones; and when you have laboriously accomplished your daily task, go to sleep in peace. God is awake.

—Victor Hugo

And he saith unto them, Why are ye fearful, O ye of little faith? Then he arose, and rebuked the winds and the sea; and there was a great calm.

—Matthew 8:26

God, you are my rock and foundation. When the storms of life rage around me, I know that I can seek warmth and security in your loving grace. You are a beacon guiding me through the thick fog of fear and confusion to the safe comfort of the shore. Steady and true are your love and your strength. Steadfast and secure am I in the light of your changeless and timeless presence that permeates the darkest of nights.

I'm not afraid of storms, for I'm learning how to sail my ship.

—Louisa May Alcott

Far better it is to dare mighty things, to win glorious triumphs, even though checkered by failure, than to take rank with those poor spirits who neither enjoy much nor suffer much, because they live in the gray twilight that knows not victory nor defeat.

—Theodore Roosevelt

O God of comfort, make me resilient like the sandy beach upon which the waves crash. Make me strong like the mighty willow tree that bends but does not break in the high winds. Give me the patience and wisdom to know that my suffering will one day turn to a greater understanding of your ways, your works, and your wonders.

Let suffering swell and subside on its own, like the natural rhythm of the ocean waves upon the steadfast shore.

Be patient with everyone, but above all with yourself...do not be disheartened by your imperfections, but always rise up with fresh courage. How are we to be patient in dealing with our neighbor's faults if we are impatient in dealing with our own?

—St. Francis de Sales

Wait on the Lord: be of good courage, and he shall strengthen thine heart: wait, I say, on the Lord.

—Psalm 27:14

*L*ord, thank you for calling me to yourself and then giving me your Spirit to strengthen me—heart, soul, mind, and body—to work in ways that bring honor to you. This goal of being a model of good works in every respect makes me realize how much I need you each moment. And as I grow in a life of doing what is right and true and good, help me grow in humility as well, remembering that you are the source of my strength.

Be strong and of a good courage; be not afraid,
neither be thou dismayed: for the Lord thy God is
with thee whithersoever thou goest.

—*Joshua 1:9*

*L*ord, you're never missing in action—you're with me all the time, everywhere, without fail. Please keep this knowledge in the forefront of my mind today so I'll be encouraged and emboldened to move through each challenge without feeling intimidated, fearful, or ashamed. In your name, I pray.

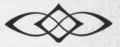

*G*od, I take comfort in the knowledge that you will never give me more than I can handle. I do ask you though to give me the strength and courage to handle what you've given me. I am grateful to be alive, but

I could use some help right now in dealing with these feelings of anxiety and doubt. Give me the promise of your everlasting comfort so I may take that with me no matter what dark or stressful path life takes me down. You will be the lamp that guides my steps and warms my heart.

He giveth power to the faint; and to them that have no might he increaseth strength.

—Isaiah 40:29

God of the strong and the weak, the brave and the fearful, I come before you to place myself in your loving hands. Take my broken places and make them whole. Heal my wounds that I might be strong for you. Give me patience to accept your timing, and help me to trust in your goodness. In your gracious name, I pray.

I am weak, but thou art mighty; hold me with thy powerful hand.

—William Williams

I ask in prayer today for courage and strength to face some big challenges before me. I admit I am anxious, and even afraid, but I know in my heart you will never give me anything I cannot handle, and that you will be by my side the whole way. Instill in me a strong heart and spirit as I deal with my problems and keep my mind centered and focused on the solutions you set before me. I ask nothing more than your presence alongside me as I overcome these obstacles and learn the lessons each one has for my life. I thank you, Lord of comfort, for always being there for me in my times of need and struggle.

In the aftermath of tragedy, it takes energy and courage to rebuild. How amazing that your gift of courage translates worry into energy and fear into determination. Help us recognize ill feelings as potential fuel that can be turned into reconstruction tools. Through your grace, we've courageously faced what was our lives and we are now off to see what our lives can be.

It takes moral courage to grieve. It requires religious courage to rejoice.

—Søren Kierkegaard

Almighty Lord, overseer of all that exists,
do you see the needs of the poor and displaced
children of the world? I know you do, Lord, but
I sometimes wonder how you can allow them to
live without safe water to drink or shelter from
the raging storms and blazing heat. Comfort them,
Lord, and if my discomfort when I think of them
is a sign that there is something I can do to help,
I am willing. Show me the way.

Fear thou not; for I am with thee: be not dismayed;
for I am thy God: I will strengthen thee; yea, I will
help thee; yea, I will uphold thee with the
right hand of my righteousness.

—*Isaiah 41:10*

Lord, please be my strength. When I am scared, please make me brave. When I am unsteady, please bring your stability to me. I look to your power for an escape from the pain. I welcome your comfort.

ℒife is filled with experiences that require us to reach deep within and find our courage. When fear threatens to keep us from trying something new, we can tap into that inner courage, which is God's presence, and find our footing. We may still be afraid, but we go forward anyway, knowing we will be given all we need to take on the challenge and tackle any new situation.

When my own strength fails me, I turn to God. When my heart quivers in fear, I turn to God. When I am scared and don't know what to do next, I turn to God. There are times when my own strength is enough, but when it isn't, I know that God is always present to pick me up when I fall and carry me. With God at my side, my fear vanishes and my courage returns.

It was high counsel that I had once heard given to a young person, "Always do what you are afraid to do."

—Ralph Waldo Emerson

*G*od, grant me the courage to let go of shame, guilt, and anger. Free me of all negative energies, for only then will I become a conduit for joy and a channel for goodness.

*B*eing human means being weak at times, and it is nothing to be ashamed of. Living requires a lot of courage, and when we don't have enough to get us through, we can always turn to one who does. That one is God. Our weakness is his strength, and our fear is his courage. With God, all things are possible and we are always protected, guided, and loved.

Chances are you limit yourself in life because of fear and doubt. But God says you can do all things through him. God strengthens you and empowers you to break through those limitations and experience a joyful life. Even if you are afraid, go ahead and do it anyway and you will find God there to give you wings to soar with.

In my hours of weakness, I reach out to others for the strength to carry on. In my times of need, I ask for help from others, and their love gives me the courage to keep going. God has given us the gift of other people not just to love us, but also to be there for us when we cannot make it on our own.

Know how sublime a thing it is
To suffer and be strong.

—Henry Wadsworth Longfellow

One of the greatest gifts in life is being able to be there for someone who is suffering. Sharing our strength, hope, and courage with those that are feeling weak is a blessing for all involved. The gift of service in the form of being someone else's pillar of strength, something they can lean on when their own legs fail them, is such a powerful experience of love in action.

$\mathcal{F}$eel the fear and do it anyway, for you will find you have more inner strength than you ever imagined. Call upon God to be there, should you fall, and go ahead and try. You may find out that you had the ability to do it alone all along, but isn't it good to know that when you can't, God is there to back you up?

Chapter 4
God's Guidance

I will instruct thee and teach thee in the way which thou shalt go: I will guide thee with mine eye.

—*Psalm 32:8*

God of all comfort, I know that with you by my side I am never alone. Your perfect love casts out all fear, doubt, and uncertainty. Your presence emboldens and empowers me. You are the light that guides me to safety again.

Father, I realize that even people of faith have different struggles with discouragement and depression. It's a relief to realize that I'm not the only one. But where do I go from here? I need your wisdom and guidance. I guess praying is the best place to begin. Just being reminded that you are near keeps me from the despair of feeling alone, and it's comforting to feel so heard and understood when I'm talking with you. I need you to help me through this day, Father. Just this day. I'll take them one at a time with you.

When I feel my control slipping, Lord, I know I only have to call on you for encouragement, direction, and guidance to get your loving assistance.

If we live in the Spirit, let us also walk in the Spirit.

—*Galatians 5:25*

Lord, how we cling to your promise that the Holy Spirit is always near to all who believe in you. How comforting it is for us as parents to know that our children have the Holy Spirit to guide them and lead them into a purposeful life. We praise you, Lord, for your loving care for us and for our children.

And be not conformed to this world: but be ye transformed by the renewing of your mind, that ye may prove what is that good, and acceptable, and perfect, will of God.

—*Romans 12:2*

Guide us, dear God, to the perfect destiny you have set out for us. Help keep us on the path to right action, right choices, and right solutions to the problems we may encounter. Help deliver us from obstacles that may detour us and lead us astray. Show us the way to fulfill your divine plan.

Our worries are hard to dismiss, Lord of comfort. They seem to grow bigger and bigger until they take over our lives. Please help us conquer them, one at a time. Your reassurance is welcome. Amen.

Shew me thy ways, O Lord; teach me thy paths.

—*Psalm 25:4*

I have such good intentions, Lord Almighty, but sometimes I slip in carrying them out. Guide my actions so that they match my words as I make footprints for others to follow. Make me worthy of being a pathfinder.

*For this God is our God for ever and ever:
he will be our guide even unto death.*

—*Psalm 48:14*

Dear God, even though I feel alone, I know you are always with me. Your loving hand guides every step I take. Knowing that you will never leave me brings me such comfort. I cannot see the road ahead, but you can, for you know all the dangers and obstacles. If I put my trust in you, you will keep me safe, protecting me from my enemies and from my own weakness. Please be with me, now and forever. Amen.

Savior, like a shepherd lead us,
Much we need thy tender care;
In thy pleasant pastures feed us,
For our use thy folds prepare.
Blessed Jesus, blessed Jesus,
Thou hast bought us, thine we are.
Blessed Jesus, blessed Jesus,
Thou hast bought us, thine we are.

—Dorothy A. Thrupp

*Thou shalt guide me with thy counsel, and
afterward receive me to glory.*

—*Psalm 73:24*

God, I give thanks for the wisdom you share with me when I am trying to understand my own actions or someone else's. You know what is best, and you have my highest good in mind. I will turn to you for the advice and guidance I need. Thank you, God, for being a strong and comforting presence in my life.

*Wherefore take unto you the whole armour of God,
that ye may be able to withstand in the evil day,
and having done all, to stand.*

—*Ephesians 6:13*

*L*ord, be my warrior, my guard, and my guide. Let your love be the armor that shields me from the slings and arrows of the day. Let your compassion be the blanket that protects me from the cold at night. Lord, be my warrior, my champion, and my protector. Let your love surround me like an impenetrable light that nothing can break through to do me harm. Let your grace bring me peace no matter how crazy things are all around me. Lord, be my warrior.

Teach me to do thy will; for thou art my God: thy spirit is good; lead me into the land of uprightness.

—Psalm 143:10

*W*hen we struggle in unfamiliar territory, Lord of comfort, we feel your calming, guiding hand and remember that you have always been faithful to your children. Then we know that our journey is safe. Please continue to give us confidence as we move to where you are calling us.

*But now, O Lord, thou art our father; we are the clay,
and thou our potter; and we all are the work of thy hand.*

—*Isaiah 64:8*

O God, you created us, and you know us better than we know ourselves. You also love us more than we love ourselves—and more than anyone on this earth loves us! Resting in that truth, I know that it's easier to turn our lives over to you. When we need to be redirected, we trust you to do the redirecting. When we're bent out of shape, we want you to be the one to straighten us out again. And if things ever get so bad that you need to humble us and remold us, even then we place ourselves in your hands. For what you create by your hands is always more magnificent than what we can design ourselves.

When I leave you behind and try to go about my day without your guidance, God, it's like groping around in the dark. I stub my heart on relational issues. I trip over my ego. I bump into walls of frustration. I fall down the steps of my foolish choices. How much better to seek the light of your guidance first thing and enjoy the benefit of having you illuminate each step of my day!

And my people shall dwell in a peaceable habitation, and in sure dwellings, and in quiet resting places.

—*Isaiah 32:18*

O Holy Creator, who hath bound together heaven and earth, let me walk through your kingdom comforted and protected by the warm rays of your love. Let me be healed as I stand basking in the divine light of your presence, where strength and hope and joy are found. Let me sit at rest in the valley of your peace, surrounded by the fortress of your loving care.

Then the word of the Lord came unto me, saying, Before I formed thee in the belly I knew thee; and before thou camest forth out of the womb I sanctified thee, and I ordained thee a prophet unto the nations.

—Jeremiah 1:4–5

Dear Lord, you knew me in my mother's womb. You set my path before me, and you watch me every moment from sunup to sundown and from sundown to sunup. I need not fear any trial that I may encounter in this world because you have already written all the days of my life. All I need to do is place my trust in you and walk obediently in faith. As long as I have you to guide me, I will prevail because your holy mercy has already saved and delivered me. Amen.

$\mathcal{O}$ God, all the instruction and guidance we need to live a purposeful life is provided for us in your Word. So why do we find ourselves allured by commentators on talk shows or by self-help gurus with all the latest and purportedly greatest approaches to life's problems? Keep me in your perfect will for my life, God, and prevent me from being pulled this way and that by all the influences this world promotes. For I know that it is only when you are leading me that I am moving in the right direction.

He shall feed his flock like a shepherd: he shall gather the lambs with his arm, and carry them in his bosom, and shall gently lead those that are with young.

—Isaiah 40:11

I know that when I wander from you, dear God, you always come and get me. Like a loving shepherd watching over his flock, you gently nudge me back in the right direction to keep me from harm. Sometimes I admit I refuse to listen to those nudgings, and yes, I get into some form of trouble because of it, but then, dear God, you always turn my attention back to you and the loving guidance you offer me. Thank you for being my shepherd, my guardian, and my heavenly Father. Amen.

He shall call upon me, and I will answer him: I will be with him in trouble; I will deliver him, and honour him.

—*Psalm 91:15*

*C*onfusion is directing my thoughts. My mind loyally follows its erratic demands and becomes increasingly lost and frustrated. I need a sign to orient myself and to find my way out of this turmoil. Find me, Lord, for I am wandering in the wilderness of my own mind, heading deeper and deeper into despair. Where are you? I call. And then I realize that by describing my lostness, you show me where I am and how to return home.

And we know that all things work together for good to them that love God, to them who are the called according to his purpose.

—Romans 8:28

O God, though you are silent today, I believe you will answer my prayers for guidance and help. I'm sure that you have heard my pleas, and you know what my heart desires, but more than that, you know what is best for me. I am willing to wait until I hear your voice and until your meaning is clear to me. I will have patience, for I have faith that all things happen according to your plan.

L ord, the best way I know to say thank you for your wonderful guidance is to try to be the kind of person you have taught me to be. Please continue to lift me up every day as I strive to be my best self.

And the Lord said, I have pardoned according to thy word: But as truly as I live, all the earth shall be filled with the glory of the Lord.

—Numbers 14:20–21

A man's heart deviseth his way: but the Lord directeth his steps.

—Proverbs 16:9

O may thy spirit guide my feet
In ways of righteousness;
Make every path of duty straight,
And plain before my face.
Amen.

—Joachim Neander

*My soul thirsteth for God, for the living God:
when shall I come and appear before God?*

—Psalm 42:2

O God, my days are frantic dashes between have to, ought, and should. There is no listening bone in me. Lead me to a porch step or a swing, a chair, or a hillside, where simply sitting can restore me. With you there to meet me, sitting places become prime places for collecting thoughts, not to mention fragmented lives.

There are questions we cannot answer, and problems we cannot find solutions for, when we only look with our eyes. But when we look from the heart, asking God for guidance and direction, we see those answers and find those solutions. Our vision is limited. God alone is unlimited, and he speaks through the heart.

The road of life is rockier when we rely on our own will and listen to our own thoughts. Our egos get in the way, clouding our vision and often leading us down paths we aren't meant to walk, with people we aren't meant to walk with. By putting our trust in God, we come to rely on his guidance alone, letting him decide who is to be a part of our lives, and how.

Think of God's presence as an internal GPS system guiding you to your destination. God knows the quickest and easiest routes to get you where you want to go, despite your efforts to try your own way, which usually results in detours and in roadblocks. Let God dictate the way, and relax in knowing you will arrive where you need to be, when you need to get there.

Walk in the light! So you shall know
that fellowship of love.
His Spirit only can bestow,
who reigns in light above.
Walk in the light! And you shall find
your heart made truly his,
who dwells in cloudless light enshrined,
in whom no darkness is.
Walk in the light! And yours shall be
a path, though thorny, bright.
For God, by grace, shall dwell in thee,
and God himself is light.

—Bernard Barton, adapted

I am the good shepherd, and know my sheep,
and am known of mine.

—*John 10:14*

*Y*our Word says—and I've heard it elsewhere—that a flock of sheep knows its own shepherd's voice and won't respond to the voice of a different shepherd. It's true of my relationship with you, too, Lord. I know your voice. I know when you're speaking to my heart, and I know when I'm being coaxed by "other voices"—wrong desires, worldly values, anxiety, pride, and the like. Thanks for helping me see the difference. Coax me to follow the sound of your voice today and always.

$\mathcal{I}$ go into prayer and ask God what to do. His answers may not come immediately, but they do come and are always the wisest choices. Because God is all-knowing, I can look to his guidance and not rely on my own limited perceptions. I pray to God for help, and then wait upon the guidance I need. It never fails me.

If you feel lost and alone, and don't know where to turn or what to do, just ask God to show you the way. Not only will God guide you in the right direction, but walk beside you, giving you courage and comfort as you find your way again. You are never really lost with God in your life. He loves you and always knows what is best for you.

Think of the times in your life when you felt like everything was going wonderfully, as if there were a master plan and all the pieces of the puzzle were falling into place. Chances are, you were following God's guidance and moving towards his will for you, instead of resisting and fighting it. Life flows so much better when we go with God. He sees the dreams of our hearts, and knows best how to fulfill them.

$\mathcal{L}$ife is a series of paths that you must choose to walk. It's hard to know which one will bring you the happiness you seek, and sometimes you have to change direction in the middle of the road. By asking God for guidance, you can find your way much easier. There will still be obstacles and the temptation of trying out other roads, but by staying in God's guiding will, you won't be led astray.

*I*f I am confused about what choice or decision to make, I turn to God. If I am not able to solve a problem that is making my life difficult, I turn to God. If I feel as though nothing is going right, I turn to God. I turn to the only one who possesses the wisdom and insight to best direct me. People can help me, but God alone guides me.

I will lift up mine eyes unto the hills, from whence cometh my help. My help cometh from the Lord, which made heaven and earth.

—*Psalm 121:1–2*

*L*ord, why is it that when the struggles, challenges, and hurts of life press in upon me, even my physical presence is downtrodden? In times of trial and grief I sometimes feel as if I'm just struggling through quicksand with my head bowed and my eyes downcast. But you, O Lord, are the lifter of my head. In time, I realize that looking down won't solve anything, but looking up will. Lord, I look to you for your guidance.

He maketh me to lie down in green pastures:
he leadeth me beside the still waters. He restoreth
my soul: he leadeth me in the paths of righteousness
for his name's sake.

—*Psalm 23:2–3*

Thank you, Lord Jesus. Thank you for walking beside me on days when I'm too hurried and frazzled to think clearly. Thank you for softly saying to me, "Slow down. It's just not worth it." Thank you for reminding me that even you drew away from the demands of the world to rest and spend time with your heavenly Father. If you needed that kind of restoration, certainly I do, too. You and you alone can calm my spirit and restore my soul, and I want to listen and respond when you lead me away from the fray.

God, thank you for sometimes reminding me that in the center of chaos lies the seed of new opportunity and that things are not always as awful as they seem at first. I often forget that what starts out bad can end up great and that it is all a matter of my own perspective. Amen.

Chapter 5
Finding Forgiveness

Blessed are they whose iniquities are forgiven, and whose sins are covered.

—*Romans 4:7*

$\mathcal{C}$omfort me in my day of need with a love that is infinite and true. Ignore my lack of desire to forgive and forget. Fill my anger with the waters of peace and serenity that I may come to accept this situation and move on to a greater level of understanding and knowing.

$\mathcal{F}$orgiveness includes letting go of the little things. Keeping a growing account of the small misdeeds of others in our memory bank is a formula for relational bankruptcy. Accumulating offenses, rather than forgiving them, feeds resentment and anger, and it chokes out our ability to love. "Forbearing one another, and forgiving one another,"

Paul taught; "even as Christ forgave you, so also do ye" (Colossians 3:13). Choosing to forgive people—even for the littlest things they do that hurt or annoy us—is vital for enjoying life and love.

*H*eavenly Father, teach me to forgive others their transgressions and to let go of angers and resentments that poison my heart and burden my soul. Teach me to love and understand others and to accept them as they are, not as I wish they would be. Amen.

Let your anger set with the sun and not rise again with it.

—Irish Proverb

He that cannot forgive others, breaks the bridge over which he himself must pass if he would ever reach heaven, for everyone has need to be forgiven.

—George Herbert

Be ye kind one to another, tenderhearted, forgiving one another, even as God for Christ's sake hath forgiven you.

—Ephesians 4:32

*L*ord, it's hard to mend a friendship when trust has been broken. And yet when we open your Word, we see how you continued to love your people even when they abandoned you again and again! Give us that same ability to love and forgive in the face of broken trust, Lord. Heal our relationships as only you can.

An apology is a friendship preserver, an antidote for hatred, never a sign of weakness; it costs nothing but one's pride, always saves more than it costs, and is a device needed in every home.

—Author Unknown

Wherefore I say unto thee, Her sins, which are many, are forgiven; for she loved much: but to whom little is forgiven, the same loveth little.

—Luke 7:47

My great God, you have told us over and over in the Bible that to love is to forgive. Help me spread love to those around me through my unquestioning forgiveness of their transgressions, real and imagined. Help me to stop "keeping score," and to remember that we are to love endlessly, just as you love us. It is when I love others that I bring your kingdom to this earth. Amen.

In whom we have redemption through his blood, the forgiveness of sins, according to the riches of his grace.

—*Ephesians 1:7*

Dear Jesus, you have given us the greatest gift imaginable through your birth and death—the gift of salvation. You have rescued us from despair and hopelessness by dying to atone for our sins. The forgiveness you have brought to our lives is the most precious gift we could ever hope for. Today, let me revel in the glory of redemption and know that I am saved, for this world and for all eternity. Amen.

Confess your faults one to another, and pray one for another, that ye may be healed. The effectual fervent prayer of a righteous man availeth much.

—James 5:16

My Lord, you have commanded us to forgive each other. It's not a suggestion, but an order, and I am struggling to carry it out. My own spirit will not be ready for absolution until I have granted forgiveness to those who have trespassed against me. As long as I hold anger and bitterness in my heart, I am separating myself from your love. Please make my spirit humble and ready to forgive so that I may receive your mercy. Amen.

Lord, your forgiveness, based on your love for me, has transformed my life. I've experienced inner healing and freedom in knowing that you have wiped my slate clean and made me your friend. Help me to become an extension of your love to those around me. Let healing happen as I apply the salve to the wounds they inflict on me. Please strengthen me while I carry it out in your name. Amen.

The longer I live, the more I realize how much forgiveness I need from you, how much we all need. My hidden sins of pride, envy, malice, hypocrisy, and greed are no less spiritually deadly than promiscuity, lying, adultery, and murder. There are no "safe" sins. They may have different consequences in the context of society, but they all cost you the same painful price when you reached out to offer forgiveness to all who would receive it. I have, indeed, been forgiven much. May my love for you and others reflect that I truly understand this.

When others harm us, there is a path to healing that should include confession by the guilty party, actions that restore where possible, and a change of behavior that demonstrates genuine repentance. Meanwhile, whether or not the other party does what is right, we can choose to forgive. Instead of choosing retaliation or revenge, we can extend love and compassion. This doesn't mean that we coddle them or fail to confront any hurtful ways, but it does mean that even as we hold them accountable, we don't withhold our love.

To be forgiven is to be absolved of all the charges of guilt and responsibility. To forgive is more freeing still. It is release from a prison of your own making.

God of all comfort, we simply couldn't survive in a world without forgiveness. If we had to carry our sins around like rocks in a bucket, how many of us could even make it to the end of the driveway? But your forgiveness lightens our load. Because of you, we can cast off the sins that weigh us down and move freely through the life you created for us to live. "Thank you" seems so inadequate when expressing gratitude for such a powerful gift as forgiveness. Please look into our hearts and see the fullness of our gratitude there. May it honor you.

*H*eavenly Father, I never fail to come to you for help and comfort in the dark times of my life, yet I don't always remember you when my cup is overflowing. Forgive me if I seem ungrateful and take your generosity for granted. How can I forget all that you give me each day? You bring beauty, peace, comfort, and love to my existence. My heart overflows with thanksgiving.

God, please forgive those in the world who know not what they do. Their hearts have grown cold as stone, and they have no love for themselves or for others. I pray for them—these people who do harm to others—that they may somehow find hope and see the light again and that even as they sin and sin again, they will be forgiven. No human is a waste of life, and I ask that the light of your love and compassion melt their hearts and that your mercy and your forgiveness set them free.

They who forgive most
shall be most forgiven.

—William Blake

I acknowledge my sin unto thee, and mine iniquity have I not hid. I said, I will confess my transgressions unto the Lord; and thou forgavest the iniquity of my sin.

—Psalm 32:5

*H*eavenly Father, I know I need you not only to forgive my sin but also to forgive the guilt I feel because of it. When I feel guilty, I keep dredging up my sins as if they weren't really forgiven. I'm so sorry if that insults and offends you, Father. You have told me again and again that I am forgiven. I thank you with my whole heart for not only forgiving me but also for taking away the guilt of my sin.

Come, Thou long-expected Jesus,
Born to set thy people free;
From our fears and sin release us;
Let us find our rest in thee.

—Charles Wesley

If we confess our sins, he is faithful and just to forgive us our sins, and to cleanse us from all unrighteousness.

—*1 John 1:9*

O Lord, how grateful I am that, because of your love for me, you have cleansed me of my sin and offered me the gifts of forgiveness and salvation with open arms. Never fail to nudge me when I am starting down the wrong path, Lord. I know your corrections are better than the world's consequences.

*L*ord, sometimes my past rises up to haunt me—or worse yet, to bite me. These are the real-world consequences of poor choices I've made. But even though I'm reminded of them because of the cause-and-effect nature of things, once I confess them to you and receive your forgiveness, they are erased from your record book. So even when I'm reminded of my old sins in one way or another, help me to quickly let go of any guilt or shame that rears its ugly head. While consequences may linger, your forgiveness is complete. Thank you for that eternal reality.

*L*ord, I need you to help me with the concept of forgiving people over and over again for the same behavior. I know you taught that there was no limit to the number of times we should forgive someone, but I get so weary of doing it, Lord. Help me to have a heart of forgiveness, so ready to forgive that I do so before the person who has wronged me even seeks my forgiveness. There's freedom in that kind of forgiveness, Lord. Help me claim it for my own.

If thou, Lord, shouldest mark iniquities, O Lord, who shall stand? But there is forgiveness with thee, that thou mayest be feared. I wait for the Lord, my soul doth wait, and in his word do I hope.

—Psalm 130:3–5

At times I tend to compare myself with other people, dear Lord, thinking I'm better or worse than this person or that person. How futile those thoughts are! Especially when I consider that we're all sinners in need of your forgiveness. It kind of levels the playing field to think in those terms. I'm so glad that with you there is forgiveness. If there wasn't, what would we all—what would *I*—do? Please cause my reverence for you to grow as I humbly accept your amazing gift of mercy— a forgiveness big enough for everyone.

As far as the east is from the west,
so far hath he removed our transgressions from us.

—Psalm 103:12

O Lord, when you promise us you have removed our sins from us, why do we dredge them up so we can wallow in regret and shame all over again? Keep us from wasting time and energy thinking about past mistakes, Lord. If they are no longer on your radar, they surely don't belong on ours. How blessed we are to have such a compassionate, forgiving God!

Dear Lord and Father of humankind,
Forgive our foolish ways;
Reclothe us in our rightful mind,
In purer lives Thy service find,
In deeper reverence, praise.

—John Greenleaf Whittier

Forgiveness is the fragrance the violet sheds on the heel that has crushed it.

—Mark Twain

My supreme Lord, give me a forgiving heart. When someone unintentionally ignores me or hurts my feelings, let me respond with forgiveness before they are even aware of the wrong. In these and other situations, I pray that forgiveness will become an automatic response for me—not something I have to consciously work on. I guess what I'm really asking, Lord, is please give me a heart like yours. Only then will I be able to live a life full of spontaneous forgiveness.

And of Benjamin he said, The beloved of the Lord shall dwell in safety by him; and the Lord shall cover him all the day long, and he shall dwell between his shoulders.

—*Deuteronomy 33:12*

O Comforter, have mercy on me. I got angry today with my wife and accused her of not helping me enough. I scolded my child for talking too much. I shouted at the dog for barking too loud. And I almost hung up on my brother for taking up too much of my time. I need your comforting strength, God, wrapped around me like a soothing blanket, so that I can ask my family for forgiveness. Bless me with more patience, too, so that we don't have to go through all this again tomorrow. Thank you, God.

God forgives me all of my sins and transgressions. In return, I am to forgive those who sin against me. This is hard to do, because it's so much easier to hold onto grudges and resentments, even over trivial things. I feel that I was right and just, and that they hurt me. But until I can let go of that, I will never be free to be happy. God forgives me, and I must forgive others in return.

Holding onto anger poisons the spirit. We must learn to let go and let God remove the anger so that we can feel free. Release the burden to God through forgiveness. Just because we forgive doesn't mean we condone the behavior, just that we no longer allow it to control us. Give it to God. Forgive.

For thou, Lord, art good, and ready to forgive; and plenteous in mercy unto all them that call upon thee.

—*Psalm 86:5*

*H*ow blessed we are to have the mercy and forgiveness of God! No matter what we do, God is ready to love and forgive us. This doesn't mean we go out and purposely do wrong, thinking we will get away with it, but we are human, and we do make mistakes now and then. Knowing that God won't abandon us when we do keeps us humble.

To forgive someone is the highest form of compassion. To try and understand that another's actions might have come from their own anger or struggles means we are empathic towards our fellow humans. God forgives us and offers his compassion. Why would we not do the same to our fellow humans?

Do not worry about the regrets of the past. God forgives you. Do not stress over a wrong word or a misguided action. God forgives you. Do not cry over a bad decision or a terrible mistake. God forgives you. Learn the lessons from your actions, then turn to God and know that he loves you and forgives you. Then strive to do better the next time.

If I forgive someone, I am not doing it just for that person, but for myself. The weight of holding onto things that have been done to me dampens my spirit. When I forgive, that weight is lifted and I no longer feel connected to what was done to me. The person I forgive is free as well. It's all about letting go of the things that drag me down so I can live the life God intended.

The act of forgiveness is promised by God to never go unacknowledged.

We have all been hurt in life. We have all been at the receiving end of another's wrath or anger. Even if that person never apologizes, we must still forgive. Do we want to live our lives holding onto the actions of another? Do we want to feel the tension of another person's behaviors towards us? It is only when we forgive that we can once again feel light and loving and kind.

The brave and compassionate soul can forgive the most horrible of crimes. With God's love and guidance, we can forgive much less. People hurt people, and God asks that we look beyond the surface of things to the deeper truth. We are all God's children, even those that do terrible things, sometimes causing us tremendous pain and suffering. Forgive them anyway.

Confessing our sin to God is like bursting into cool, refreshing air after being stuck a long time in a stifling, hot room. It frees our soul from the suffocating misery of pride, guilt, and pretense. Best of all, "coming clean" about our wrongdoing is the way back to right relationship with God. His merciful love grants us the forgiveness we so desperately need.

O Lord, your willingness to forgive is astounding! You've never done anything wrong, and yet you are ready to forgive those who have sinned against you whenever they sincerely confess and turn away from the wrong they've done. I want to thank you for being so merciful toward me, for forgiving my debt of sin. I will always praise you for your goodness in dealing with me so gently. Help me to remember to be merciful toward others, just as you have been toward me.

To err is human, to forgive divine.

—Alexander Pope

Chapter 6

Words of Love

Love comforteth like sunshine after rain.

—*William Shakespeare*

For thy mercy is great above the heavens:
and thy truth reacheth unto the clouds.

—Psalm 108:4

*H*is love is wider than our worries, longer than our loneliness, stronger than our sorrows, deeper than our doubts, and higher than our hostilities. This is why valleys are so wide, rivers so long, winds so strong, oceans so deep, and the sky is so high. With these, we can have a picture of the wonder of his love.

*L*ord Jesus, it is so easy to seek comfort from material things, like a new car or sofa. But you are not found in worldly things. The only true source of everlasting comfort is your love, the living water you offer us from your very lips. Let me remember to seek first your will, perfect and divine. It is only then that my weary heart will rest and find sanctuary. Amen.

But as many as received him, to them gave
he power to become the sons of God, even to
them that believe on his name.

—John 1:12

$\mathscr{L}$ord, you are the only one we need. Like a little child who wakes up crying in the middle of the night, cold and scared, we long to be comforted. But you wrap your arms around us and keep us safe in the shelter of your love. And so we come to you as desperate children again and again, wanting nothing more than to gaze into your face and receive your comfort. Thank you for the promise that we are your children forever and that when we come to you for comfort, you will never turn us away.

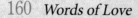

Loving, like prayer, is a power as well as a process. It's curative. It is creative.

—Zona Gale

One word frees us of all the weight and pain in life. That word is love.

—Sophocles

God, I thank you for the blessing of the love of good friends. Each day my friends shower me with love and care, and I feel comfort knowing they are always there for me. I am so grateful for each one of them, as different and unique as they are, and for the things they teach me. My friends are like gemstones, so priceless and beautiful. Thank you for old friends and new friends and for friends yet to come.

There is a comfort only God can provide, a food for the soul and drink for the heart that quenches all sense of emptiness and aloneness. All too often, we seek comfort in things outside of ourselves, in the confines and limitations of the material world. But there already exists a comfort that needs no seeking; it needs only recognition. God's love fills us, but we have to acknowledge its presence within. God's comfort holds us in arms strong and caring, all knowing and wise, but we have to quiet our anxious minds to feel them wrapped around us. We must first silence the inner chatter that forever looks outside of itself for what it already has, and has had all along.

...in all human sorrows nothing gives comfort but love and faith.

—Leo Tolstoy, Anna Karenina

Love is faith, and faith, like a gathered flower, will live rootlessly on.

—Thomas Hardy

God did not make us to walk through life alone, but to do so with the ones we love and care about. To love others, and have the experience of their love in return, is the highest expression of God's own love through us, his children. We reach out to others in friendship and find that we are never as alone as we thought.

I can tell you love me, Lord! I feel your presence today as I work. I see your answer to last week's prayer right before my eyes. I feel my spirit lifted when I sing praises to you as I drive in the car. You are behind me, before me, and within me. Wherever I go, I am surrounded by your love—love that has no bounds and knows no end. Thank you, Lord. All I can say is, "I love you, too!"

If we are willing to receive them, the messages of love God sends us are more comforting, uplifting, inspiring, moving, delightful, and assuring than the words of a thousand silver-tongued poets, preachers, or paramours.

$\mathcal{D}$ear Lord, my heart is feeling empty today, and I long for a true love to come into my life. Help me to become the kind of person I look for in another, a partner and companion that will walk with me through life. Send me a love I can trust and believe in, who will stand up for me when the world threatens to push me down. I believe that you have created someone special just for me, so please prepare me to receive that special person so that we may be together soon. Amen.

*In the multitude of my thoughts within
me thy comforts delight my soul.*

—*Psalm 94:19*

Dear God, I know that your comfort comes in all shapes and sizes. My pets offer me unconditional love that helps lift my spirit. Being around creatures so happy to see me soothes my pain and reminds me how important I am to other living things. God, I know you work in mysterious ways, and some of those ways involve four padded little paws that imprint love directly upon my heart.

And above all things have fervent charity among yourselves: for charity shall cover the multitude of sins.

—1 Peter 4:8

The height to which love exalts is unspeakable. Love unites us to God. Love covers a multitude of sins. Love beareth all things, is long-suffering in all things. There is nothing base, nothing arrogant in love. By love have all elect of God been made perfect.

—Clement of Rome

May be able to comprehend with all saints what is the breadth, and length, and depth, and height; And to know the love of Christ, which passeth knowledge, that ye might be filled with all the fulness of God.

—*Ephesians 3:18–19*

They say all you need is love, and that is true, God. Your loving care has gotten me through so many lumps and bumps, and you continue to be there for me at each and every turn on the road of life. My heart shines with the love that never ceases, the love of you, my God, who always watches over me and makes clear my way. You take away my burdens and lighten my load, and your love smoothes the path you have set out for me. Thank you, God.

God loves each of us as if there was only one of us.

—*St. Augustine*

I know, O Lord, that thy judgments are right, and that thou in faithfulness hast afflicted me. Let, I pray thee, thy merciful kindness be for my comfort, according to thy word unto thy servant.

—*Psalm 119:75–76*

Father God, as we journey through life, remind us of your comforting presence. Let us see your love in everything and everyone. Amen.

*H*oly One, I have striven to do what is right in your eyes. I have followed your Word and obeyed your laws to the best of my ability. I now ask that you love me and comfort me. My needs are great and my power is small, but in you all things are possible. Please remove my burdens from me, for they are too heavy to carry without your help. Soothe me, love me, and care for me. Amen.

And the second is like, namely this, Thou shalt love thy neighbour as thyself. There is none other commandment greater than these.

—*Mark 12:31*

*L*ord, it has been said that it is better to give than to receive, and in no case is this more true than in the ability to love others. My heart fills with joy when I can offer support, share my skills or knowledge, or simply just be with someone in pain. This ability to love others is a gift from you, and is but a taste of what awaits us in heaven. Thank you for giving us a glimpse of your kingdom, and thank you for allowing me to become part of your good works on Earth.

*Beloved, let us love one another: for love
is of God; and every one that loveth is
born of God, and knoweth God.*

—1 John 4:7

Holy God, you have shown me light and life. You are stronger than any natural power. Accept the words from my heart that struggle to reach you. Accept the silent thoughts and feelings that are offered to you. Clear my mind of the clutter of useless facts. Bend down to me, and lift me in your arms. Make me holy as you are holy. Give me a voice to sing of your love to others.

Dear Lord, I feel like I've been waiting forever for a true friend to share my life with. There are so many times when I feel alone in this big world. I want a companion to walk with, laugh with, and share hopes, fears, and disappointments with. Please help me find someone I can trust and love. And until I find that person, please remind me that I am never really alone because I have you, unconditionally and eternally. Amen.

*God's love for us is
complete and constant.*

Joy is love expected;
peace is love in repose;
long-suffering is love enduring;
gentleness is love in society;
goodness is love in action;
faith is love on the battlefield;
meekness is love in school;
and temperance is love in training.

—Dwight L. Moody

And Jesus looking upon them saith,
With men it is impossible, but not with God:
for with God all things are possible.

—Mark 10:27

*L*ord, could you please help me to love the unlovable? I know it's not possible for me to do this alone, so allow me to see them through your eyes—as precious people created in your image. I know that in some ways we all look the same to you, Lord, even as you are so keenly aware of our differences. To you, we are all lovable. Give me eyes to see others that way too, Lord. Without you, it's simply not possible.

Love has hands to help others. It has feet to hasten to the poor and needy. It has eyes to see misery and want. It has ears to hear the sighs and sorrows of men. This is what love looks like.

—St. Augustine

And thou shalt love the Lord thy God with all thy heart, and with all thy soul, and with all thy mind, and with all thy strength: this is the first commandment.

—Mark 12:30

*L*ord, I truly want to love you with all my heart, soul, mind, and strength—so why do I have such a hard time doing it? At times my heart is fully engaged in loving you, but my mind is struggling with unanswered questions. Some days my soul seems too weary to love, Lord, and my strength? Well, it's just not there. Forgive me, Lord. It is my dearest desire to love you as totally as you deserve to be loved. Help me even in this, Lord.

$\mathcal{D}$ear Father, when I was a child, I went to my mother for comfort. She held me in her lap, rocked me close to her heart, and wiped my tears away. As I grew older, suddenly I was the parent and had no one to turn to for shelter. That is when I learned that you are my loving Father, my Abba, who will always hold me close, just as my mother once did. No matter how old I grow, I can still feel the safety of a child held in loving arms, comforted and loved beyond all measure. I know that I am yours, a child of God, who you know by name and love for all eternity. Amen.

There is no greater comfort to a broken spirit than the love of God. There is no more soothing a balm to heal the wounds of a suffering soul than the love of God. There is no deeper peace to be found for a restless heart than the love of God.

When I am having a bad day, and the last thing I want to do is love, I love anyway. This is when God calls upon me the most to get out of my bubble and give comfort to someone else who might need it. In turn, I begin to feel more loving, towards myself, towards others, and towards humanity. God knows that the best way to find the love we seek is to give it.

Loneliness can sometimes feel like a thick, heavy fog blocking out the warm sun and blue sky. But remembering that God loves me helps clear away the fog and gives me a new sense of clarity and direction. Even if people cannot find time for me, God is always there, unfailing in his love and steadfast care.

Love has the power to heal all wounds, calm all troubled souls, and comfort all lost spirits. Love alone can turn a life around and give a renewed sense of peace and joy to a heart that was sure it was broken forever. Love frees the mind of doubt and fear. Love goes into dark places and enlightens. Love attempts the impossible and makes it possible.

The world is filled with unloving people, but God asks that we love them anyway. It does no good to meet hatred with more hatred, so God asks that we meet hatred with love. The more good we can put into the world, the better our world will be, and soon that goodness will spread like wildfire, changing cold hearts to warm, and lost souls to found again. That is the power of love.

A heart in pain from disappointment can't always see the love that already surrounds it. That love is ever-present because it comes from God, who never abandons us. The love of God is steady and true, even when we think nobody cares about us. God does, now and forever. Opening our hearts to God is the beginning of healing, and the end of pain and suffering. God's love abides in us...always.

Four stages of growth in Christian maturity
Love of self for self's sake
Love of God for self's sake
Love of God for God's sake
Love of self for God's sake.

—St. Bernard of Clairvaux

*J*ust for today, look around at all the love the world has to offer. Just for today, forget your worries and allow yourself to give love to the world in return. Just for today, surrender your fears to God's everlasting love. Just for today, remind people that you love them and let them love you back, even if you don't feel lovable. Just for today, let love be who you are.

God comforts me with his love when I am feeling cold and alone. God warms me with his loving care when I am feeling neglected. God sees me when I am feeling unseen, and reminds me of my worth when I am feeling inadequate. God's love is my comfort in all things, and it makes me whole again.

I hold it true, whate'er befall;
I feel it, when I sorrow most;
'Tis better to have loved and lost,
Than never to have loved at all.

—Alfred, Lord Tennyson,
"In Memoriam"

Under his wings I am safely abiding,
though the night deepens and tempests are wild;
still I can trust him, I know he
will keep me,
he has redeemed me and I am his child.
Under his wings, under his wings, who
from his love can sever?
Under his wings my soul shall abide,
safely abide forever.
Under his wings, O what precious enjoyment!
There will I hide till life's trials are o'er;
sheltered, protected,
no evil can harm me,
resting in Jesus I'm safe evermore.
Under his wings, under his wings, who
from his love can sever?
Under his wings my soul shall abide,
safely abide forever.

—William O. Cushing

God, of all your precious gifts, love is the rarest and most precious of all. Too often I find myself acting in ways that are unloving and unkind. That is when I most need your love to remind me to stop and take a deep breath. Anger and hatred never solve any problems. Only love seems to make the rough spots smoother and the hard roads easier to walk upon. I ask that you continue to remind me of the power of love each day, especially when it seems so much easier to choose to be unkind.

Greater love hath no man than this,
that a man lay down his life for his friends.

—*John 15:13*

God, they say you get by with a little help from your friends, and I know that to be true. Thank you for filling my life and my days with good friends who care about me. Each one is like an angel sent down from heaven in human form, and I cherish them all. So today I ask that you keep my friendships strong and true, no matter how much time or distance may separate us as we all live our separate lives. Keep them close where it counts—in my heart. Thank you.

Yet, in the maddening maze of things,
And tossed by storm and flood,
To one fixed trust my spirit clings;
I know that God is good!...
I know not where His islands lift
Their fronded palms in air;
I only know I cannot drift
Beyond His love and care.

—John Greenleaf Whittier,
"The Eternal Goodness"

Love is greater than faith, because the end is greater than the means. What is the use of having faith? It is to connect the soul to God. And what is the object of connecting man with God? That he may become like God. But God is Love. Hence, Faith, the means, is in order to Love, the end. Love, therefore, obviously is greater than faith. "If I have all faith, so as to remove mountains, but have not love, I am nothing."

—Henry Drummond

*H*ow often do we let time drift by without telling those we hold dear to us how much we love them? How often do we fear speaking words of love because we might be rejected? If only we could possibly know just how much we are loved, by each other, and by God. We would then know that miracles truly exist and all things are possible. Love gives us wings. Tell someone you love them today.

Chapter 7
God's Grace

For the Lord God is a sun and shield:
the Lord will give grace and glory:
no good thing will he withhold from
them that walk uprightly.

—*Psalm 84:11*

$\mathcal{G}$od's grace is our comfort in times of trouble and our beacon of hope amid the blackness of despair. By opening ourselves to God's ever-present grace, we know we are loved and cared for, and our hearts sing out in joyful gratitude.

My grace is sufficient for thee: for my strength is made perfect in weakness. Most gladly therefore will I rather glory in my infirmities, that the power of Christ may rest upon me.

—2 Corinthians 12:9

$\mathcal{G}$racious God, of all the gifts you give us, grace may be the most glorious! With your unmerited favor falling upon us, we can survive most anything. In times of plenty or of want, your grace is sufficient.

When we feel so exhausted we don't know how we'll get through the morning, let alone the day, your grace is sufficient. And when serious illness strikes or death is imminent, your grace is sufficient. Thank you, God, for your marvelous, glorious gift of grace.

Now our Lord Jesus Christ himself, and God, even our Father, which hath loved us, and hath given us everlasting consolation and good hope through grace.
—*2 Thessalonians 2:16*

Dear God, your heavenly grace has rescued me from the darkness and brought me into the light again. Each time I'm reminded of your miraculous presence in my life, the light gets brighter and problems melt away. I know then that you have touched me with a special, loving touch that makes my heart sing out with joy just to be alive. Knowing that you deem me worthy of your grace renews my strength and hope that all will be well in my life. Thank you, God.

O God, I know you will never give us a burden to bear without giving us the grace to endure it, but some burdens just seem so heavy we find ourselves wondering if they can be survived. I ask that you send an abundant amount of strength and grace to all those who suffer so. Let them feel your presence in a very real way, God, for without you, they have no hope. I ask this in Jesus' name. Amen.

Heavenly Father, your grace can refresh and renew us with the living water of hope and faith. Please help us fully live the lives you have given us.

Trust the past to God's mercy, the present to God's love, and the future to God's providence.

—*St. Augustine*

For by grace are ye saved through faith;
and that not of yourselves: it is the gift of God:
Not of works, lest any man should boast.

—*Ephesians 2:8–9*

*L*ord in heaven, your grace is given to me as my birthright in Jesus Christ. Yet still I find myself hardening my heart against others, thinking that they do not "deserve" my kindness or my time. What a hypocrite I am! Nothing I have ever done has made me worthy of your sacrifice to me—the one who is ever willing to judge others. Please forgive me for my pride, and help me open myself to all my brothers and sisters. I ask in the holy name of Jesus Christ. Amen.

Almighty God, how sweet your amazing grace is to my soul! Like a healing balm from above, you soothe my fears and comfort my worried heart. Your presence is a candle that no wind can blow out. Your wondrous grace is ever-present and is an infinite light that guides me always to you. When your grace appears in my life, I know that I am always cared for and watched over by the one who loves me most. Your sweet, amazing grace is the gift of your love—a love that knows no boundaries or limitations.

For the law was given by Moses, but grace and truth came by Jesus Christ.

—*John 1:17*

Christ is no Moses, no exactor, no giver of laws, but a giver of grace, a Savior; he is infinite mercy and goodness, freely and bountifully giving to us.

—*Martin Luther*

My Lord, I'm feeling terribly down today. My heart is broken, and nothing seems to be going right. I don't mean to complain, but I'm really unhappy. I need your loving grace to remind me that there's a rainbow that follows the storm and that night always gives way to the dawn. When I'm in this painful place, I cannot see the light. Darkness surrounds my thoughts and my emotions. Please reach out your hand and help me climb out of this lonely place and into a brighter new perspective on my life and my future. Grant me your grace by revealing your loving presence, Lord. Amen.

O most merciful Lord, grant to me thy grace,
that it may be with me, and labour with me,
and persevere with me even to the end. Grant
that I may always desire and will that which
is to thee most acceptable, and most dear.
Let thy will be mine, and my will ever follow
thine, and agree perfectly with it. Grant
to me above all things that can be desired,
to rest in thee, and in thee to have my
heart at peace.

—Thomas à Kempis

We don't know when grace will happen, or even how it will show up in our lives, but if we have faith in God, his grace will appear just when we need it the most, reminding us that we are children of a loving Father who will never let us down and is always on our side.

Move our hearts with the calm, smooth flow of your grace. Let the river of your love run through our souls. May my soul be carried by the current of your love, towards the wide, infinite ocean of heaven. Stretch out my heart with your strength, as you stretch out the sky above the earth. Smooth out any wrinkles of hatred or resentment. Enlarge my soul that it may know more fully your truth.

—*Gilbert of Hoyland*

Then will I sprinkle clean water upon you, and ye shall be clean: from all your filthiness, and from all your idols, will I cleanse you. A new heart also will I give you, and a new spirit will I put within you: and I will take away the stony heart out of your flesh, and I will give you an heart of flesh. And I will put my spirit within you, and cause you to walk in my statutes, and ye shall keep my judgments, and do them.

—Ezekiel 36:25–27

Heavenly Father, your grace washes over me today, taking away all my impurities. I praise your name as I revel in your love. I can feel my soul shining as I turn my face to you. Please let me soak in the promise of eternal life in you, as I feel it penetrate my body to the very core. I want to carry that promise with me always, so as soon as I close my eyes, I can sense your Holy Spirit wrap around me, holding me safe. I ask in the name of your precious Son, Jesus Christ. Amen.

O God, in all I do, I want to honor you. Fill me with your grace so that I can release it into the world with each task I undertake and each person I touch. I have little to offer on my own, God, only the skills and gifts you created in me. But filled with the Holy Spirit and your grace, there's no limit to the impact my life can have. Use me, God! I want to be an ambassador of your amazing grace.

I have seen his ways, and will heal him:
I will lead him also, and restore comforts unto
him and to his mourners.

—*Isaiah 57:18*

Gracious God, this loss I now grieve threatens to consume me. I have never felt so much sadness and hopelessness. Let your loving grace encompass me in comforting warmth, like a blanket that shuts out the cold. My heart breaks, and my spirit is weak. Turn your face upon me and help me get through this trying time. Also, help those who also suffer from loss. In you, we find merciful comfort. In you, we find a home and shelter from the pain. In you, God, we rest our weary souls and find the strength we need to rise up and face our suffering. Thanks be to you, loving God.

What is God's grace? It is the breath of God upon my face and the touch of God upon my heart, gently moving me in the right direction. What is God's grace? It is the whisper of love in my ear and the comfort of warmth on my skin, promising that the cold, dark night is at an end. What is God's grace? It is the laughter of a child and the hugs of a friend, lifting my spirit higher. What is God's grace? It is the presence of God, who is kind, good, and loving, and to whom I can always turn.

*Grace be with all them that love our
Lord Jesus Christ in sincerity. Amen.*

—Ephesians 6:24

God of comfort, where do I turn when my life seems to be in a state of total upheaval? When family and job and health are all askew and nothing seems to be working out right? Please comfort me like a parent comforts a child, rock me in your loving arms, and whisper that it will all be better tomorrow. In your heavenly grace I will find the rest I need to face the new day with the wherewithal to handle anything set before me. Your comfort is the soothing balm I need right now to ease my worry and my fears. Thank you, God of comfort.

Faith is a living, daring confidence in God's grace. It is so sure and certain that a man could stake his life on it a thousand times.

—Martin Luther

I know that when I am sad, lonely, and afraid, I can turn to God for his loving grace. With mercy and compassion, God hears my cries and comes to my aid, ready to take away my burdens and heal my wounded heart. He gives me wisdom and understanding, and helps me to forgive those who have hurt me. God's unceasing love for me is what grace is all about.

*L*iving in grace means loving with compassion. When we open our hearts to others, even those we call our enemies, not only do they benefit, but we do as well. They get the joy of feeling our loving energy surround them, and we get the happiness that comes from knowing we have touched others with the same grace God offers us.

$\mathcal{S}$urrender to the grace of a loving God. Give up your worries and concerns, your fears and doubts, to a God that cares and won't let you down. Turn over your challenges and obstacles to a God who makes your way clear and smooth again. When life becomes a struggle, give up the fight and give in to the grace of a power greater and wiser than yourself.

$\mathcal{W}$e think of grace as God's favor upon us, but God is always favoring every single one of us. Grace is the acceptance of that favor, allowing it to flow through our days and nights, bringing the gifts of a comforting God to us whenever we need it. Grace, like God, is a door through which we must first walk to enter a room filled with blessings, love, and joy.

There but for the grace of God go I. God is my protection, and my guardian. I know that I am always being watched over and blessed because that is God's promise to me. I walk in grace, and offer it to those I meet along the way. I stand in grace, letting it surround me with a love that is eternal and forgiving of all my sins.

$\mathcal{M}$y God, I fill my days with tasks and activities to give me status in the eyes of men and women, but I'm missing the most important fact: That because of your grace, nothing I can do can make you love me more or less. Meanwhile, help me seek your approval, not the approval of this fallen world. Let me take time from the "doing" to simply be with you, releasing myself and my life to you and your will more and more each day.

The grace of the living God refreshes like cool, clear water on a hot day, giving our parched souls the sustenance and nourishment they need.

$\mathcal{G}$race is the presence of God at work in your life. It shows itself in the form of people and events that come into your orbit just when you need them. Small miracles and happy coincidences are proof that God is always showering grace down upon you. Just open your eyes, and your heart, and you will see it everywhere.

Like sun that melts the snow,
my soul absorbs the grace
that beats in gentle, healing rays
from some godly place.
Like rain that heals parched earth,
my body drinks the love
that falls in gently, soothing waves
from heaven up above.

*L*ord, today I ask you to slow me down and open my ears so I will notice the needs of those around me. Too often I breeze by people with an offhand greeting but remain in a cocoon of my own concerns. I know many around me are hurting, Lord. Help me find ways to be a comfort to others.

*Comfort your hearts, and stablish
you in every good word and work.*

—*2 Thessalonians 2:17*

*He that does good for good's sake seeks
neither praise nor reward, but is sure
of both in the end.*

—*William Penn*

*L*ord, when all else fails I know that I can count on you to be my fortress. I give thanks each day for the steadfast comfort you provide, and I pray that you will give this same comfort to those who suffer in fear and silence today. Give to them the same freedom from worry as you did me, by showing them the same mercy and love you show me each day. Be their fortress just as you are mine so that they, too, may understand they never walk alone.

Who comforteth us in all our tribulation,
that we may be able to comfort them which are in
any trouble, by the comfort wherewith
we ourselves are comforted of God.

—*2 Corinthians 1:4*

God promises us his comfort, but he also uses us as his agents to comfort others. In fact, the difficulties we've gone through often give us the ability to reassure others who are now going through the same experiences. How will God use you to extend comfort to someone else?

Great Comforter, never let our need overshadow our recognition of the needs of others. Ground us in empathy. Commission our sympathy. Urge us to offer comforting hands and understanding hearts. And in so doing, show us how easing the pain of others eases our own.

Teach me to feel another's woe,
To hide the fault I see;
That mercy I to others show,
That mercy show to me.

—Alexander Pope

God, let me be a comfort to someone who needs me today. As you have always comforted me in rough times, let me do the same for someone who is sad, ill, or suffering and needs to know they are cared for. Guide me toward those I can be of loving service to, and let no opportunity pass me to do something good in the world today. If someone is in need, send him my way. If someone is depressed, have her call me. Let me be a comfort to those who feel they cannot go on alone. I am at your service today, God. Make use of me. Amen.

And to esteem them very highly in love for their work's sake. And be at peace among yourselves. Now we exhort you, brethren, warn them that are unruly, comfort the feebleminded, support the weak, be patient toward all men. See that none render evil for evil unto any man; but ever follow that which is good, both among yourselves, and to all men.

—*1 Thessalonians 5:13–15*

We have been created to love each other, to help each other, and to heal each other. In doing so, we love, help, and heal ourselves.

Lord, today I ask you to bless and comfort all who daily see pain and desperation as part of their jobs. Bless the doctors and nurses working with the seriously ill, and comfort them with your insight. Bless and comfort the caretakers toiling through the night, Lord, and send your strength to restore them. All these people are serving you as they serve others. Please give them your special blessing, Lord of comfort. Amen.

Doing nothing for others is the undoing of one's self. We must be purposely kind and generous, or we miss the best part of existence. The heart that goes out of itself gets large and full of joy. This is the great secret of inner life. We do ourselves the most good when we are doing something for others.

—Horace Mann

$\mathcal{L}$ord Jesus, I pray for comfort for all those in need. There are so many hurting, bleeding souls in this fallen world, and only the balm of your presence can ease their suffering. Please be with all those whose hearts cry out for your love and mercy. Your power is great, your spirit is awesome, and the bounds of your generosity know no limits. You alone can provide refuge to these lost ones who need you but do not yet know you. I entreat your will, Lord. Amen.

And I will pray the Father, and he shall give you another Comforter, that he may abide with you for ever.

—John 14:16

Dear heavenly Father, today, if I see or hear of someone who is struggling in some way, please help me take a moment to remember what it was like when I was struggling and you comforted me through the aid of a friend or stranger. Let that memory mobilize me to offer comfort and be your true servant. This I pray. Amen.

*Comfort ye, comfort ye my
people, saith your God.*

—*Isaiah 40:1*

There is no greater joy than being able to provide comfort to someone who is going through a rough time. Our love serves to soothe their pain, and our attention allows them to release the weight of their suffering. All we need to do is be there and listen, the way God listens to our prayers and our tears when we need comfort. We can be angels to others in need.

God is our comforter when life overwhelms us. Imagine being able to help someone else who might be feeling overwhelmed! We should never think we aren't capable of being helpful to others. God's love is within us and all we need to do is let it flow out in compassion, empathy, and care. God calls upon us to be there for others as he is there for us.

I know I can count on my friends and family to provide the comfort I need when I am sick or depressed. They do their best to be there, and I return the love and attention. But now and then I need something more. I need God's special brand of comfort and loving care. God's love goes bone-deep and warms the coldest corners of my frightened heart. God's love fills the darkest corners of my broken spirit. And for that I am truly grateful.

There's a reason why our arms are made the length they are. God made them that way to provide hugs filled with love and warmth to those who feel lost and alone. Often that is all someone needs—to be acknowledged, listened to, and held awhile. Caring for others does not have to be big and noisy and overdone. Sometimes a hug will do.

*Grace be to you and peace from God our
Father, and from the Lord Jesus Christ. Blessed be God,
even the Father of our Lord Jesus Christ, the Father of
mercies, and the God of all comfort; Who comforteth us
in all our tribulation, that we may be able to comfort
them which are in any trouble, by the comfort
wherewith we ourselves are comforted of God.*

—*2 Corinthians 1:2–4*

God is on the job every moment of the day to give us the comfort we ask for. All he asks in return is that we give the gift of that comfort to those we come in contact with. Sometimes, it's a smile for a stranger, or a kind word for an old friend. It doesn't matter how it looks. All that matters is that we give what we get and let God perform miracles of kindness through us.

Give what you have. To some it may be better than you dare think.

—Henry Wadsworth Longfellow

*H*ow easy it is to get caught up in your own struggles that you fail to see those around you struggling, too. Yet if you reach out to them in love, they often return that love to you. Caring is contagious, and easily spread when we get out of our own heads and open our hearts to embrace those around us. This way, everyone benefits and all are comforted.

239

Chapter 9
Words of Wisdom

Wisdom outweighs any wealth.

—*Sophocles*

O gracious and holy Father,
Give us wisdom to perceive you,
intelligence to understand you,
diligence to seek you,
patience to wait for you,
eyes to see you,
a heart to meditate on you,
and a life to proclaim you,
through the power of the spirit
of Jesus Christ our Lord.

—*St. Benedict*

Who is wise, and he shall understand these things?
Prudent, and he shall know them? For the ways of the
Lord are right, and the just shall walk in them: but the
transgressors shall fall therein.

—*Hosea 14:9*

I am here right now, Father, because I do want to walk in your ways. I know the key is staying connected to you because the ways of the world are all around me, always imposing a different set of values and a different worldview. Give me a wise and discerning heart in all things today so that I can stay on track.

Through wisdom is an house builded; and by understanding it is established: And by knowledge shall the chambers be filled with all precious and pleasant riches.
—Proverbs 24:3–4

Thank you for your wise ways, Lord. Following them fills my life with true blessings—the riches of love and relationship, joy and provision, peace and protection. I remember reading in your Word that whenever I ask for your wisdom from a faith-filled heart, you will give it, no holds barred. So I'll ask once again today for your insight and understanding as I build, using your blueprints.

A wise mind knows that adverse events are blessed opportunities for growth in disguise.

Great works are performed not by strength
but by perseverance.
　　　　　　　　—Samuel Johnson

Without suffering,
there would be no learning.
Without learning,
there would be no wisdom.
Without wisdom,
there would be no understanding.
Without understanding,
there would be no acceptance.
Without acceptance,
there would be no forgiveness.
Without forgiveness,
there would be no joy.
Without joy,
there would be no love.
Without love,
there would be no life.

For the commandment is a lamp; and the law is light;
and reproofs of instruction are the way of life.

—*Proverbs 6:23*

$\mathcal{L}$ord of all, your Word is so alive—so vibrant—
that it almost seems illuminated when I am reading
it. When I am troubled, opening the Bible is like
turning on a comforting light in a dark, gloomy
room. Thank you, Lord, for loving us so much that
you gave us your wisdom to illuminate our lives.

He is like a man which built an house, and digged deep, and laid the foundation on a rock: and when the flood arose, the stream beat vehemently upon that house, and could not shake it: for it was founded upon a rock.

—*Luke 6:48*

*D*ear Lord, help me to build on a firm foundation by relying on your wisdom, diligently seeking your direction in all I do, learning to walk in your paths of kindness, peace, and justice to my fellowman. In Jesus' name, Amen.

*F*aith, as sturdy as the stone foundation beneath a century-old house, forms the bedrock upon which I stand, unswayed despite the winds of change.

251

The glory of young men is their strength: and the beauty of old men is the grey head.

—Proverbs 20:29

*L*ord, time and again I see that you intend for the generations to go through life together. The joy the youngest child brings to the eldest grandparent is such a blessing to all who witness it. Even when it isn't possible for us all to be together all the time, let us see the wisdom in sharing our lives. Please keep us ever alert to the unique gifts each generation has to share.

*S*ometimes it's amazing how much you can learn from your children.

$\mathscr{L}$ord, help me understand that the challenges I am going through serve to empower me. Teach me the wisdom to discern that my trials mold me into something far grander than even I could have imagined. Amen.

Knowledge stops at the edge of the earth. Faith goes beyond the stars, illimitable, calm, all-comprehending. The wisdom of the world is a surface wisdom and breeds only a surface humor. The wisdom of faith reaches from heaven to hell, into the heart of all living; and when it smiles the angels of God smile with it.

—Reverend F. X. Lasance

God may throw us a few curves in life—we may feel hassled, troubled, anxious, or uncomfortable, and not understand why our circumstances don't fit our desires. But if we trust in the wisdom of his plan, God will provide for all our needs.

Having knowledge is not the same as having wisdom. The true test of wisdom is knowing how and when to act, according to God's will.

We don't receive wisdom; we must discover it for ourselves after a journey that no one can take for us or spare us.
—Marcel Proust

*T*hink of each problem you encounter as nothing more than a challenging reminder from God to think a little higher and reach a little farther. When met with a difficult situation along the road of life, greet it, acknowledge it, and move past it. Then you will be able to continue on your journey a little stronger, a little wiser.

*L*ord, sometimes it's hard for us to discern the difference between brave, courageous actions and foolish, faulty ones. Often we rush ahead with a plan we think is from you only to watch it end in disaster. At these times we know we moved too fast. Yet we don't want to lack the faith to move forward when necessary! Give us wisdom and discernment, Lord. Let the courageous spirit you instilled in us fuel actions that bring you glory.

The most productive classrooms don't always consist of four walls and a roof. An appropriate climate for learning may be sitting on green grass under a blue sky. It may be a garden swing and a good book. It may be nothing more than a mind deep in thought.

Facts can be taught in a day;
wisdom lasts for a lifetime.

Even a fool, when he holdeth his peace, is counted wise:
and he that shutteth his lips is esteemed a
man of understanding.

—Proverbs 17:28

*L*ord, teach me to think ahead about the results my actions might inflict. If things go awry despite my forethought, help me admit my wrongs and right them. Amen.

The fear of the Lord is the beginning of wisdom: a good understanding have all they that do his commandments: his praise endureth for ever.

—*Psalm 111:10*

*L*ord, so often I keep doing the same things over and over and getting the same unsatisfying results. This is when I need for you to shine your light on my life and reveal to me all that I haven't been able to see through human eyes. You have all knowledge and every answer to the mysteries of heaven and Earth. Show me, Lord. Give me just a bit more of the knowledge you possess. Thank you.

Teach others what you have learned, share the lessons of your life experience, give freely from the storehouse of knowledge within, and your life will have worth and meaning.

A wise teacher seizes those unexpected opportunities to teach by experience: a caterpillar on a leaf, a bird singing in the school yard, a crack of thunder, even a dripping faucet.

What you have learned, teach others;
What you have experienced, share with others.

There is another thing that we of middle life need to guard against, and that is the loss of early enthusiasms and ideals. The tendency of life's actualities is to sober and sometimes embitter. It is a difficult thing to experience trial and failure, to see the hollowness and shame, the trickery and cruelty of the social, commercial, political world, and not get cynical and skeptical—to lose, if not your faith in God, what is next worse, your faith in man and interest in man. It is hard, in contact with the actual world to preserve your faith in an ideal world, your ardor in its pursuit. The youthful vision fades, romance gives way to prosy plodding, and life's springtime grows into the hot, dusty parched summer. Oh, men and women of riper years, let us not fail to carry our earlier enthusiasms into the dry details, the grave responsibilities of later life and make the desert places rejoice and blossom as the rose!

—Charles Sumner Hoyt

$\mathcal{I}$ may not know what the next step is, but God does. I may not understand why I am going through a particular challenge, but God does. The wisdom of God knows all and sees the bigger picture, when I am only able to grasp a small piece of the puzzle. I put my trust and faith in God's greater vision for my life and allow it to unfold according to his will.

$\mathcal{W}$hat we cannot do for ourselves, God can do for us. With our limited vision and perception, only God's wisdom can look beyond our lack and limitations. How comforting is it to know that we have this resource to turn to anytime we need? God is always ready to help us, to advise us, and to direct us.

When I am wrong, I turn within to find the right way. God's eternal wisdom is like a flowing river I can tap into at any time, especially when I am clueless and don't know which way to turn. I take comfort in knowing I don't have to be a genius and figure out every last detail of my life. God knows what is best, and as long as I stay in tune with his Word, I will be divinely inspired.

So shall the knowledge of wisdom be unto thy soul: when thou hast found it, then there shall be a reward, and thy expectation shall not be cut off.

—*Proverbs 24:14*

This world is full of people who have to be right, even if it means losing friendships or family connections. The need to be right causes so much suffering. Instead, seek the need to be wise. Seek the ability to use your God-given wisdom to be of help to others, and not a burden. No one is right all the time, and it takes wisdom to realize that and to learn to be compassionate to others, and to yourself.

Let your speech be always with grace, seasoned with salt, that ye may know how ye ought to answer every man.
—*Colossians 4:6*

That still, small voice you hear within the very depths of your soul, when the mind is calm and the spirit is quiet, is God speaking to you. Listen, for God is telling you what you need to know and do. Listen, for God is imparting wisdom that will solve your problems and overcome your obstacles. Listen, for God is giving you everything you need to be happy, if you only listen.

What does the wisdom of God sound like? Like a soft whisper from within. What does the wisdom of God look like? Signs and miracles, big and small, that point to the answers to our problems. What does the wisdom of God feel like? Like a soft, comforting blanket on a cold day that wraps around us. It sounds, looks, and feels like love.

And he said unto her, Daughter, be of good comfort: thy faith hath made thee whole; go in peace.

—Luke 8:48

Faith is the foundation upon which a happy, healthy life is built. The stronger our faith, the less our life can be shaken by outside occurrences and extraneous circumstances.

Lord, give me the faith to take the next step, even when I don't know what lies head. Give me the assurance that even if I stumble and fall, you'll pick me up and put me back on the path. And give me the confidence that, even if I lose faith, you will never lose me.

Faith in a wise and trustworthy God, even in broken times like these, teaches us a new math: subtracting old ways and adding new thoughts because sharing with God divides our troubles and multiplies unfathomable possibilities for renewed life.

Faith makes all evil good to us, and all good better; unbelief makes all good evil, and all evil worse. Faith laughs at the shaking of the spear; unbelief trembles at the shaking of a leaf, unbelief starves the soul; faith finds food in famine, and a table in the wilderness. In the greatest danger, faith said, "I have a great God." When outward strength is broken, faith rests on the promises. In the midst of sorrow, faith draws the sting out of every trouble, and takes out the bitterness from every affliction.

—Robert Cecil

*My God hath sent his angel, and hath shut the lions'
mouths, that they have not hurt me: forasmuch as
before him innocency was found in me; and also before
thee, O king, have I done no hurt. Then was the king
exceedingly glad for him, and commanded that they
should take Daniel up out of the den. So Daniel was
taken up out of the den, and no manner of hurt was
found upon him, because he believed in his God.*

—Daniel 6:22–23

God of comfort, thank
you for letting me cling
to the faith that has
sustained me through so
much uncertainty and
pain before. I now know
that although faith may
be all I have, it's also all
that I need.

*D*ear Father God, you sent your Son to us to be our Lord, to watch over us, to bring us comfort, strength, hope, and healing when our hearts are broken and our lives seem shattered. We will never be alone, not when you are here with us always and forever. Remind us to look to you for strength.

O Lord never suffer us to think that we can stand by ourselves, and not need thee.
—*John Donne*

By faith Abraham, when he was called to go out into a place which he should after receive for an inheritance, obeyed; and he went out, not knowing whither he went.
—*Hebrews 11:8*

And the Lord said, If ye had faith as a grain of mustard seed, ye might say unto this sycamine tree, Be thou plucked up by the root, and be thou planted in the sea; and it should obey you.

—*Luke 17:6*

*I*nto the bleakest winters of our souls, Lord, you are tiptoeing on tiny infant feet to find us. May we drop whatever we're doing and accept this gesture of a baby so small it may get overlooked in our frantic search for something massive and overwhelming. Remind us that it is not you who demands lavish celebrations and strobe-lit displays of faith. Rather, you ask only that we have the faith of a mustard seed and willingness to let a small hand take ours. We are ready.

*There are times in everyone's life
when something constructive is
born out of adversity . . .
when things seem so bad that
you've got to grab your fate by the
shoulders and shake it.*
—Author Unknown

*Faith makes the discords of the present
the harmonies of the future.*
—Robert Collyer

And immediately Jesus stretched forth his hand, and caught him, and said unto him, O thou of little faith, wherefore didst thou doubt?

—*Matthew 14:31*

Great Comforter, while I wait for this piercing pain of loneliness to pass, cradle me as the wailing, lost child I've become. Closing my eyes and breathing deeply, I feel your warming presence as a blanket tossed around my shoulders and know that no matter how lost I feel right now, you hold the most important truth, whispering it now: "You are my beloved child. I am with you."

*T*hrough faith we learn that the impossible is possible, that dreams can become reality, and that miracles do happen.

Sometimes I'm like Peter,
and I walk on water.
I stand above my circumstances,
which are like swirling sea tempests.
But then, like Peter,
I take my eyes off Jesus
and concentrate on things below.
Soon I start to sink.
How I long to have
a consistent, water-walking
eyes-on-Jesus faith.

$\mathcal{T}$he best way to deal with the pressures of everyday life is to patiently rely on God.

$\mathcal{W}$hen the quiet after the storm finally comes to our hearts, we look up to find that our God of comfort is still with us, holding us close to his heart.

The root of faith produces the flower of heart-joy. We may not at the first rejoice, but it comes in due time. We trust the Lord when we are sad, and in due season He so answers our confidence that our faith turns to fruition and we rejoice in the Lord. Doubt breeds distress, but trust means joy in the long run.

Let us meditate upon the Lord's holy name, that we may trust Him the better and rejoice the more readily. He is in character holy, just, true, gracious, faithful and unchanging. Is not such a God to be trusted? He is allwise, almighty, and everywhere present; can we not cheerfully rely on him? . . . They that know thy name will trust thee; and they that trust thee will rejoice in thee, O Lord.

—Charles Spurgeon

Trust in the Lord, and do good; so shalt thou dwell in the land, and verily thou shalt be fed.

—Psalm 37:3

Where there is lack, faith shouts "Abundance!" Where there is despair, faith sings out, "Joy!" Where there is fear, faith whispers "Courage." Where there is animosity, faith affirms only "Love."

Faith is love taking the form of aspiration.
—William Ellery Channing

It seems so insignificant,
this choice you have to make.
Yet the Lord can use small acts of faith
to cause the earth to shake!
So pray and wait to know his will
for decisions made today,
and the Lord may use your faithfulness
to show someone the way.

Faith offers a new way
of life, where everything
can be used for good.

$\mathcal{F}$aith is a commodity that cannot be purchased, traded, or sold. It is a treasure that cannot be claimed and put on display in a museum. It is a richness no amount of money can compare to. When you have faith, you have a power that can change night into day, move mountains, calm stormy seas. When you have faith, you can fall over and over again, only to get up each time more determined than ever to succeed, and you will succeed. For faith is God in action, and faith is available to anyone, rich, poor, young or old, as long as you believe.

For where your treasure is, there will your heart be also.
—Matthew 6:21

$\mathcal{F}$aith is neither proven through logic nor reason; it must be felt with the heart.

Therefore, my beloved brethren, be ye stedfast,
unmoveable, always abounding in the work of the Lord,
forasmuch as ye know that your labour
is not in vain in the Lord.

—1 Corinthians 15:58

Come walk with me
through life, my friend,
arm in arm we'll stroll.
With love and hope
to light our path,
and faith to guide our souls.

*T*he answers to all of life's questions lie somewhere deep inside us, and faith is the key to our knowing that the voice of our soul will guide us.

We have but faith: we cannot know;
For knowledge is of things we see;
And yet we trust it comes from thee,
A beam in darkness: let it grow.
—Alfred, Lord Tennyson

Then spake Jesus again unto them, saying, I am the light of the world: he that followeth me shall not walk in darkness, but shall have the light of life.
—John 8:12

*H*uman faith lives between two extremes, Lord: It's neither completely blind nor able to see everything. It has plenty of evidence when it steps out and trusts you, but it takes each step with a good many questions still unanswered. It's really quite an adventure, this life of faith. And Lord, I must confess that experiencing your faithfulness over time makes it easier and easier to trust you with the unknown in life. Thank you for your unshakable devotion.

*A*lthough our eyes should always be turned above toward God, sometimes we can do with a reminder of God's work just a little bit closer to home. The faith of others can serve as a reminder or an inspiration to strengthen our own faith. Just as we should provide encouragement to others, we can draw on others to help steady ourselves.

Faith is knowing without seeing,
believing without fully understanding,
trusting without touching the
Great Comforter who is ever faithful.

*T*here is a difference between wishing that
something was so and having faith that it will be.
Wishing implies an attitude of hope based on fantasy
and daydreams. Faith implies an attitude of belief
based upon reality and intentions. You can wish for a
thing all you want, but until you have complete faith
that it can—and will—be yours, it will be just a wish.

Sometimes I feel abandoned, Lord. I feel empty inside, and it's hard to connect with myself, with others, and with the world. I almost lose faith at these times, Lord. Please stay with me and help me remember your love, your light, and your peace.

Lord, how I long to stand strong in the faith! I read of the martyrs of old and question my own loyalty and courage. Would I, if my life depended on it, say, "Yes, I believe in God"? I pray I would, Lord. Continue to prepare me for any opportunity to stand firm for what I know to be true. To live with less conviction is hardly to live at all.

I am come a light into the world, that whosoever believeth on me should not abide in darkness.

—John 12:4

*L*ord, you are the light I follow down this long, dark tunnel. You are the voice that whispers, urging me onward when this wall of sorrow seems insurmountable. You are the hand that reaches out and grabs mine when I feel as if I'm sinking in despair. You alone, Lord, are the waters that fill me when I am dried of all hope and faith. I thank you, Lord, for although I may feel like giving up, you have not given up on me. Amen.

Nothing is more wonderous than faith—the one great moving force which we can neither weigh in the balance nor test in the crucible.

—William Osler

$\mathcal{F}$aith is like the wind. We hear its presence, see its power, feel its effect on the world around us. We cannot see it, but we know it is there.

I would hasten my escape from the windy storm and tempest.

—*Psalm 55:8*

$\mathcal{I}$magine having the arms of a loving, caring angel wrapped around you when you are sad or upset. Faith is like that. Comforting and encouraging, faith is like a trustworthy old friend that is never too tired or busy to hear your problems or help you find your footing again when you stumble through life. Faith in God is our best friend and ally.

What does it mean to have faith? It means moving through the challenges of daily life with boldness because we know that someone has our back. It means approaching life's obstacles with courage and conviction because we know someone is looking out for us. It means walking with our heads held high because we know someone walks with us. That someone is God.

For by grace are ye saved through faith; and that not of yourselves: it is the gift of God.

—Ephesians 2:8

Chapter 11

Hope

However long the night, the dawn will break.

—*African Proverb*

$\mathcal{L}$ike the evergreen, hope never dies, but stands tall and mighty against the coldest winter winds until the summer sun returns to warm its outstretched branches.

Nevertheless he left not himself without witness, in that he did good, and gave us rain from heaven, and fruitful seasons, filling our hearts with food and gladness.

—*Acts 14:17*

Father God, we know that to receive the blessing of healing, the heart must be open. But when we are mad, we close off the heart as if it were a prison. Remind us that a heart that is shut cannot receive understanding, acceptance, and renewal. Even though we feel angry, we must keep the heart's door slightly ajar so your grace can enter and fill our darkness with the light of hope.

He sendeth the springs into the valleys,
which run among the hills.

—*Psalm 104:10*

Each new stage draws me like bee to flower. There, hope prompts me to unfold the petals and dine on the nectar of my future.

Beautiful pastel colors,
pink, blue, golden, white,
Brightening every highway and byway,
colors soft and light.
Covering the earth in a rosy glow,
a special sunset for all to see.
Brushstrokes of heavenly beauty
on a canvas that spans the seas.
I can't describe my feelings
as I watch him paint the sky,
A sense of solace covers the earth
as another day goes by.

*There be no potion so powerful, no pill so
amazing, no promised reward so alluring as
the certain belief that something good
can happen tomorrow.*

*Be glad in the Lord, and rejoice, ye righteous: and shout
for joy, all ye that are upright in heart.*
—Psalm 32:11

Lord, you are the foundation of my life. When
circumstances shift and make my world unsteady,
you remain firm. When threats of what lies ahead
blow against the framework of my thoughts, you
are solid. When I focus on your steadfastness, I
realize that you are my strength for the moment,
the one sure thing in my life. Because of you I stand
now, and I will stand tomorrow as well, because you
are there already. Amen.

If I put my hope in people,
I am often disappointed.
If I put my hope in circumstances,
I am often let down.
But when I put my hope in God,
I am always taken care of.
God is my rock and my hope,
in him is a firm foundation
from which I live my life.
I may not always get all my
hoped-for prayers answered the
way I expect, but I get
them answered the way
God wants me to.

The promise of hope fills the heart with a new perspective, and the eyes with a new vision. Darkness begins to lift, showing the path we could not see before, and a way out of our pain and suffering. The promise of hope opens doors we were certain were closed, and reveals solutions that evaded us. Hope is a key that unlocks the way to the blessings of God around us.

Take comfort in God's steadfast presence.
Even when you suffer, take comfort
in the hope of God's healing.
Even when you fear, take comfort
in the hope of God's strength.
No matter what you face, take comfort
in knowing you never walk alone.

Chapter 12

Gratitude

---○---

Reflect on your present blessings, of
which every man has many; not on
your past misfortunes, of which all
men have some.

—*Charles Dickens*

Almighty God, what a creative God you are! Within the elements of your creation are hidden messages of wonder, encouragement, and love. A purple hyacinth breaks through the snow by a rural mailbox, and the message of hope is delivered. A single hawk swoops down and flies beside the car of someone who is grieving as if to say, "Be assured God sees your grief and is with you." A tiny kitten seems to seek the saddest person in the room and curls up in her lap. Thank you, Lord, for touching us through your creation. How very blessed we are!

In every thing give thanks: for this is the will of God in Christ Jesus concerning you.

—*1 Thessalonians 5:18*

What a wonderful day! And now, God of comfort and peace, the children are sleeping, replete with the joys of our summer discoveries that they are savoring to the last drop. We will celebrate the joy of ordinary days and rest in your comforting care.

That their hearts might be comforted, being knit together in love, and unto all riches of the full assurance of understanding, to the acknowledgement of the mystery of God, and of the Father, and of Christ; In whom are hid all the treasures of wisdom and knowledge.

—*Colossians 2:2–3*

God leaves the sun on longer in the summer so we can play more.

*If you find stumbling blocks in your path,
use them as stepping stones to move
closer to God and all that is good.*

O Lord God, this horrible disaster has really been a blow to my family and me. It was so unexpected. One day, everything is fine, and the next day, everything is gone. Our extended family, friends, and church all want to help us, and we are truly grateful for their generous compassion, but still we feel utterly defeated. A lifetime of hard work is wiped out, and now we have to start over. Please help us, Lord, to be thankful that we have our lives and each other, and most importantly, that we have you to take care of us. Help us, we pray in Jesus' precious name. Amen.

God's Word is encouraging. The psalms are a great resource for encouragement. "My soul melteth for heaviness," said the psalmist; "strengthen thou me according unto thy word" (Psalm 119:28). The psalms reveal the raw emotions of very real people who, while trusting God, were honest about their difficulties. They include poet-warriors, sage-kings, and songwriter clergy—an assortment of humanity whose joys and sorrows are chronicled, in part, for our comfort and encouragement. Whether you're singing the blues or walking on air, God wants you to know that there is a psalm to meet you where you're at—to comfort your hurting heart or to fill your mouth with thanksgiving.

Stop moaning and asking,
"Why, God, why?"
There is always a meaningful reason.
Stop whining and pleading,
"When, God, when?"
For good things will arrive in due season.
We are promised that God's never early,
But neither is God ever late.
All the blessings we wish will come to us
When we learn to have faith while we wait.
When I am lost and discouraged,
And there seems to be no hope in sight,
I turn my cares over to the God of my heart,
And his love lets my spirit take flight.

$\mathcal{L}$ord, how precious water is to us, and how parched and desperate we are when it's in short supply. How grateful we are that you promise us access to the living water that will never run dry! Keep us mindful of that refreshing supply today, Lord. Fill us up, for we are thirsty.

And the Lord shall guide thee continually, and satisfy thy soul in drought, and make fat thy bones: and thou shalt be like a watered garden, and like a spring of water, whose waters fail not.

—*Isaiah 58:11*

Gratitude may be the most highly underestimated virtue. We think of love, hope, faith, and the power of prayer and forgiveness. But how often do we stop each day and give thanks for all the blessings in our lives? Are we too focused on what we lack, what we don't have, don't want, don't need? By opening the heart and mind to focus on gratitude, we unleash a treasure of unceasing good that's just waiting to overflow into our lives. A grateful person knows that by giving thanks, they're given even more to be thankful for.

I awoke this morning with devout thanksgiving for my friends, the old and the new.
—Ralph Waldo Emerson

Know ye that the Lord he is God: it is he that hath made us, and not we ourselves; we are his people, and the sheep of his pasture. Enter into his gates with thanksgiving, and into his courts with praise: be thankful unto him, and bless his name.

—Psalm 100:3–4

Thank you, Lord, for the signs of your power. Thank you for the awe I feel during a thunderstorm or at the sight of a monument in nature. Thank you for the thrill I feel when I see one of your works in all its glory. It is good and comforting to know your power and feel its presence in my life.

*I*t's so easy to be thankful for the good. But when we encounter obstacles, how often do we curse them? Yet those difficulties are helping us to evolve into better and stronger and more loving human beings. It's easy to be grateful once the challenges are gone and we are once again in the flow of life. But try to be grateful for the hard times as well. They are very often miracles in disguise.

That the trial of your faith, being much more precious than of gold that perisheth, though it be tried with fire, might be found unto praise and honour and glory at the appearing of Jesus Christ.

—*1 Peter 1:7*

$\mathcal{W}$ake up in the morning and be grateful for the new day ahead. Every 24 hours is an opportunity to live life more fully, and love more deeply. Look at each moment and see the gift it brings. Cherish the present as it unfolds. Then, when you go to sleep at night, be thankful for the experiences God gave you. This is a life well-lived.

Give us day by day our daily bread.

—*Luke 11:3*

*But seek ye first the kingdom of God, and
his righteousness; and all these things shall
be added unto you.*

—Matthew 6:33

*L*ord, you said to first seek your kingdom and
all else will be given to me. I tried for so long
to seek those outer things first; those material
things I thought would make me happy. And all
it left me was feeling lost and alone and cold. But
the kingdom you offer is one of love, mercy, and
everlasting comfort. Your wisdom is far more
precious than rubies and more priceless than
gold. I understand that all good things can come
to me only when I first immerse myself in your
loving presence. That thought brings me a comfort
nothing outside of me ever could. Thank you, Lord.

Give to the winds thy fears
Hope and be undismayed;
God hears thy sighs and counts thy tears
God shall lift up thy head.
Through waves and clouds and storms,
He gently clears thy way.
Wait thou his time; so shall this night
Soon end in joyous day.
Let us in life, death,
Thy steadfast truth declare
And publish with our latest breath
Thy love and guardian care.

—Paul Gerhardt,
translated by John Wesley

As above the darkest storm cloud
Shines the sun, serenely bright
Waiting to restore to nature
All the glory of his light,
So, behind each cloud of sorrow,
So, in each affliction, stands,
Hid, an angel, with a blessing
From the Father in his hand.
                    —Daniel H. Howard

God of comfort, I am hurting today. All the wounds I've received in this lifetime seem open and raw, and only the balm of your love can comfort me. I need you to take me in your hands, fill me with your Holy Spirit, and ease all the aching, lonely places as only you can. I know that your power is endless and your love is merciful, and I have faith in your all-healing presence. I pray that all my worries and cares will be washed away from me, just like my sins were taken from me by the death of your son, Jesus Christ. Amen.

Create in me a clean heart, O God; and renew a right spirit within me.

—Psalm 51:10

My soul, there is a country
Afar beyond the stars,
Where stands a winged sentry
All skillful in the wars;
There, above noise and danger
Sweet Peace sits, crown'd with smiles,
And One born in a manger
Commands the beauteous files.
He is thy gracious friend
And (O my Soul awake!)
Did in pure love descend,
To die here for thy sake.
If thou canst get but thither,
There grows the flow'r of peace,
The rose that cannot wither,
Thy fortress, and thy ease.
Leave then thy foolish ranges,
For none can thee secure,
But One, who never changes,
Thy God, thy life, thy cure.

—Henry Vaughan

$\mathscr{I}$ know you will not fail to lift me up from my sorrow and gently deposit me upon the shore. And though my body is tired and my spirit is weary from weeping, I offer myself to you in complete surrender, so that you may fill my nets with the bounty of your eternal peace and the comfort of your infinite love.

*Thou shalt increase my greatness, and comfort
me on every side.*

—Psalm 71:21

Speak low to me, my Saviour, low and sweet
From out the hallelujahs, sweet and low
Lest I should fear and fall, and miss Thee so
Who art not missed by any that entreat.
Speak to me as to Mary at thy feet!
And if no precious gums my hands bestow,
Let my tears drop like amber while I go
In reach of thy divinest voice complete
In humanest affection—thus, in sooth,
To lose the sense of losing . . .
—Elizabeth Barrett Browning,
"Comfort"

O let him whose sorrow
no relief can find,
Trust in God, and borrow
ease for the heart and mind.
Where the mourner weeping
sheds the secret tear,
God his watch is keeping,
though none else be near.
God will never leave thee,
All thy wants he knows,
Feels the pains that grieve thee,
sees thy cares and woes.
Raise thine eyes to Heaven
when thy spirits quail,
When, by tempests driven,
heart and courage fail.
All thy woe and sadness,
in this world below,
Balance not the gladness
thou in Heaven shalt know.
—Heinrich Siemund Oswald,
"O Let Him Whose Sorrow"

Green grass and blossoms blanket the earth,
For spring is the season of renewal and rebirth.
Tender buds, woodland creatures,
new life without end—
How much of this do we owe to
our many angel friends?

*I*s illness your will, Lord? I need answers, for I want you to help me heal. But if you send illness, how can I trust you to heal? Reassure me that you will work everything out eventually. And when that isn't possible, be with me as I suffer. Freed from fear I can get stronger as your healing energy flows through me, restoring me to my abundant life.

Only in God do we find the blessing of renewal.

*B*lessed Creator, I long to feel a sense of unity and harmony with all that you have created. Help me understand that natural disasters are opportunities for renewal and that around every storm cloud, a silver lining waits for the one who has faith in you. Let it be.

I awoke at dawn one morning
From a restless night of sorrow,
Praying that with the daylight
Might come a bright tomorrow.
My heart as cold and hopeless
As winter's deepest chill,
I cried out for understanding
And to know my Father's will.
While treading up a garden path
Hushed in the fragrant air;
I spied a tender rose,
Its petals bowed as if in prayer.
As I gazed in silent awe,
It occurred to me—He knows!
The tears my Lord has shed for me
Are the dew upon the rose.